Stock and Options trading for Beginners

2 BOOKS IN 1

-Stock market investing for beginners

-Options trading for beginners

Gualtiero Favole

© *Copyright 2021 by Gualtiero Favole. All right reserved.*

The work contained herein has been produced with the intent to provide relevant knowledge and information on the topic on the topic described in the title for entertainment purposes only. While the author has gone to every extent to furnish up to date and true information, no claims can be made as to its accuracy or validity as the author has made no claims to be an expert on this topic. Notwithstanding, the reader is asked to do their own research and consult any subject matter experts they deem necessary to ensure the quality and accuracy of the material presented herein.

This statement is legally binding as deemed by the Committee of Publishers Association and the American Bar Association for the territory of the United States. Other jurisdictions may apply their own legal statutes. Any reproduction, transmission or copying of this material contained in this work without the express written consent of the copyright holder shall be deemed as a copyright violation as per the current legislation in force on the date of publishing and subsequent time thereafter. All additional works derived from this material may be claimed by the holder of this copyright.

The data, depictions, events, descriptions and all other information forthwith are considered to be true, fair and accurate unless the work is expressly described as a work of fiction. Regardless of the nature of this work, the Publisher is exempt from any responsibility of actions taken by the reader in conjunction with this work. The Publisher acknowledges that the reader acts of their own accord and releases the author and Publisher of any responsibility for the observance of tips, advice, counsel, strategies and techniques that may be offered in this volume.

Table of Contents

STOCK MARKET INVESTING FOR BEGINNERS

Introduction 1

Chapter 1: Why Should You Invest? 3

    Make Extra Income 3

    Planning for Retirement 4

    Earn Passive Income 4

    Achieve Financial Independence 5

Chapter 2: Fundamentals of Stock Market Investing 7

    How to Price Stocks 7

    Looking to the Future 8

    Market Organization 9

    Asset Classes 9

Chapter 3: How to Create an Investment Timeline 11

    Managing Expectations 11

    Determine the Lifestyle You Want 12

    Calculating Financial Independence 13

Chapter 4: How to Define Your Investment Strategy 15

    Buy and Hold 15

    High-Frequency Trading 16

    Value Investing 17

Setting Objectives 18

Chapter 5: Fundamentals of Day Trading 19

Definition of Day Trading 19

How to Get Started With Day Trading 20

The Best Day Trading Strategy 21

How to Determine if Day Trading Is for You 22

Chapter 6: How to Succeed at Day Trading 23

Core Strategies 23

Core Components 25

Most Successful Day Trading Strategies 26

Chapter 7: Fundamentals of Swing Trading 30

Difference Between Day and Swing Trading 30

Use Technical Analysis and Fundamental Analysis 31

Advantages of Swing Trading 32

Disadvantages of Swing Trading 33

Chapter 8: How to Succeed at Swing Trading 34

Swing Trading Strategies 34

Moving Average 35

10-Day and 20-Day Simple Moving Average 37

Moving Average Convergence Divergence Crossover 38

Breakout Strategy 39

Chapter 9: Fundamentals of Position Trading 41

Understanding Long-Term Trend 41

Advantages of Position Trading 42

Disadvantages of Position Trading... 43

Combined Strategy 44

Chapter 10: How to Succeed at Position Trading.......... 45

50-Day and 200-Day Moving Average 45

Determining Entry and Exit Points 47

Pullback and Retracement Strategy 47

Resistance Levels and Breakouts 50

Chapter 11: Value Investing... 52

Determining Intrinsic Value.. 52

Determining Market Value 53

Spotting Potential Value 53

Setting Up Your Trade 54

Conclusion.. 56

OPTIONS TRADING FOR BEGINNERS

Introduction 1

Chapter 1: History Of Options Trading............................ 2

Olive Harvest And Thales 2

Tulip Bulb Mania Of The 17th Century 3

Brokers And Russell Sage 4

Chapter 2: Basics Of Options 6

What Are Options? 6

Options And Its Advantages 8

Options And Its Disadvantages 9

Styles Of Options 9

Exotic Options 10

Chapter 3: Choosing Brokers 12

Opting For Free Education 12

Testing The Broker's Customer Service 13

Ensuring That The Trading Platform Is Simple To Use 13

Proper Assessment Of Breadth, Costs, And Depth Of Data And Tools 14

Not Weighing The Price Of Commission Heavily 15

Trading Platforms 16

Chapter 4: Management Of Risk 18

Opting For A Trade Plan 18

Management Of Risk Using Options Spreads 20

Management Of Risk Using Diversification 21

Management Of Risk Using Options Orders 22

Money Management And Position Sizing 22

Chapter 5: Covered Calls 24

Basics Of Covered Call 25

How Can You Profit From Covered Calls? 25

When Is The Right Time To Sell Covered Calls? 26

Chapter 6: Putting Into Use The Collar Strategy 27

Collar Strategy In Detail 27

Break Even Point And Collar Profit Loss 28

Example Of Collar 29

Forecasting Market 29

Chapter 7: Call Spreads 31

Bull Call Spread 31

Bear Call Spread 33

Calendar Call Spread 35

Chapter 8: Put Spreads 37

Bear Put Spread 37

Bull Put Spread 40

Chapter 9: Common Mistakes Of Beginners 42

Focusing On OTM Options 42

No Proper Exit Plan 43

Not Being Attentive To Small Gains For The Huge Gains 43

Not Paying Attention To Written Options 44

Chapter 10: Having The Right Mindset 45

Improving Your Mindset 45

Chapter 11: Psychology Of Trading 49

Quick Decisions 49

Understanding Fear 49

Dealing With Greed 50

Developing Rules 51

Conclusion 52

STOCK MARKET INVESTING FOR BEGINNERS

Introduction

Welcome to "*Stock Market Investing for Beginners. The Ultimate Guide to Creating a Profitable Portfolio.*" This is the beginning of an exciting journey that will lead you to become financially independent. In the following pages, you will uncover the secrets the stock traders and financial experts know but don't want to share with you. Herein, you'll find a treasure trove of insider secrets. If you believe there is a magic formula for making money investing in stock, you'll find that all it takes is the right know-how.

Throughout this book, we will discuss the information you need to know. We will dispense with the fluff and focus on the meat and potatoes. You will get the real information on how to make money, thereby creating a solid financial life for you and your family.

We are going to delve into the secrets of day trading. If you are keen on rolling up your sleeves, day trading is the right approach for you. You'll find out how you can make money day trading, from the comfort of your home and office, and without having to work more than you already do.

We are also going to look into swing trading. This trading approach is highly profitable. However, you need to know when to strike. In doing so, you'll be able to cash in on market opportunities that don't come around very often. But when they do, you will be ready for them.

We are going to discuss position trading. This is a long-term trading strategy that will allow you to maximize your returns. This is where you hit home runs. They take time to set up. But once you have the right deal in place, it can be very rewarding for you. As such, position trading is the ultimate approach for high-value investors.

If this sounds too good to be true, then stick around to learn how you can make the most of your time and effort. You are surely interested in investing as you are looking for the best way to help your family be financially secure.

You can't guarantee your family's financial wellbeing by taking on another job. Nor can you become financially independent by working longer hours. This is the reason why stock investing is so appealing. Plenty of other folks out there have made stock investing work for them. Now, it's your turn to make some real money.

Ultimately, you can continue to live your usual life knowing that you have all of your bases covered. You can afford to continue your day job, not because you have to, but because you want. This is the type of freedom that can come from stock market investing.

The secrets are here.

Once you see them in action, you will realize that it's simple to achieve. However, the right know-how is essential to making things work for you. So, buckle up because we are going to cover a lot of information. Rest assured that the information we will discuss is presented in a clear and concise form.

Thanks again for choosing this book, make sure to leave a short review on Amazon if you enjoy it, i'd really love to hear your thoughts!

Let' get down to business!

Chapter 1: Why Should You Invest?

To invest, or not invest? That is the question.

When you think about investing, what comes to mind?

For most people, the idea of investing is very similar to gambling. They roll the dice on a stock, win big, and solve all of their problems. However, this is something seen in the movies but not in real life. In real life, investing is a carefully planned action. By taking the time to carefully plan investments, returns are often much greater than expected.

Therefore, investing is something that we need to see as an opportunity. If you look at investing as pain today, fun tomorrow, then you will never make it. When you commit to investing because you know you will achieve your objectives, then you are well on your way to making some serious cash.

So, let's take a look at the reason why you should invest.

Make Extra Income

The majority of folks that invest do so to supplement their current income. It's hard to make a decent living from just one income stream. Moreover, it's hard to make money by working longer hours. Therefore, most people look for other means of supplementing their monthly income.

This is where investing comes into play.

When you invest money, you eventually get paid returns on your investments. Typical investment vehicles such as mutual and index funds pay interest on a monthly or quarterly basis. They provide additional funds that can be put toward any number of purposes. However, the returns you can get from these investments are often underwhelming.

Many times, the returns you get from mutual funds can be disappointing. This is the reason why lots of people look toward investing directly into stocks. By cutting out middlemen, investors stand to make far better gains. As such, savvy, proactive investors use day, swing, and position trading as a way of generating regular income. When you come to combine your regular income plus income from investing, you have a winning formula that can help you fund a comfortable lifestyle.

Planning for Retirement

This is a long-term approach. Investment accounts such as IRAs and 401(k)s provide a way of financing expenses during retirement years. These investments work very well for folks who have time to spare. Thus, the younger you get started, the more money you stand to make. By the same token, the longer you take to open one of these accounts, the less time you have to fund your retirement.

Therefore, investing in stocks makes sense for those looking to save up for retirement. Depending on your strategy, you can simply roll over investment to make your nest egg grow. Over time, you'll not only have a regular income but also a substantial amount of capital racked up. As a result, stock investing makes perfect sense for those saving up for retirement.

Earn Passive Income

Passive income is one of the most intriguing reasons to invest. Passive income basically means you don't actively work for the income you earn. This may sound too good to be true, but it is a fact. When you invest in stocks, you can set up your trading system to do the work for you. Nowadays, virtually all trading is done through computers. There is algorithmic trading you can use to help you automate all of your transactions. Consequently, all you need to do is set up your trades and let the system handle the rest.

By taking advantage of automated trading, you can devote a couple of hours a day, or a week even, to your trades. Once you have everything set up, you can sit back and watch the action. Of course, you need to stay on top of the action. But doing so won't require you to spend hours in front of the computer.

Also, there are folks who choose to make trading a full-time job. If you choose to do so, you can work both actively and passively. You can set up trades to work automatically while you focus on other directly. In a way, you are conducting multiple trades at once.

If you have ever wondered how stockbrokers make so much money in a short time frame, this is the answer. They use the power of automated trading to do multiple transactions at once.

Achieve Financial Independence

Financial independence means that you don't need to work to finance your lifestyle. In other words, you choose to work. You work because you want to, not because you have to. This is the true meaning of freedom. Additionally, this is not something that you can achieve by working a job.

People who become financially independent achieve this by investing in stocks, real estate, or business ventures. They reach a point where they have regular income without actively working. Therefore, they don't need to work a 9 to 5 routine to make money. They have an automated system that works for them.

When you achieve financial independence, you can afford to make time for the things you have always wanted. You can provide for your loved ones without having to sacrifice your time. You can prioritize your health rather than work. In the end, financial independence is the ultimate goal most people seek.

The truth is that most people say they want to be rich. What they mean is that they don't want to worry about paying the bills every month. What most people really want is to have a comfortable life in which they can afford to do whatever they want, whenever they want. Thus, they are not obsessed with a specific amount of money in their bank account.

Now, if you are keen on becoming truly wealthy, then you can certainly achieve this through stock investing. It takes time and patience, but it pays off in the end. The principles in this book will help you get there. But you need to start investing today. The longer you wait, the longer it will take you to get to the promised land.

Chapter 2: Fundamentals of Stock Market Investing

To be successful in the stock market, you need to understand the nuts and bolts that hold it together. Generally speaking, the stock market functions like any other market. There are buyers and sellers that come together to agree on a price. As such, price is the ultimate mechanism by which investors can carry out transactions.

So, let's discuss how the market prices stocks.

How to Price Stocks

The core element of pricing stocks is supply and demand. In short, when there is high demand (lots of buyers) and low supply (few sellers), then price goes up. In contrast, when there is low demand (few sellers) and high supply (lots of sellers), price goes down. If sellers and buyers are equal, then there is a perfect market price. This is the general rule that's applied to all commodities in a free market. Unless a market is manipulated, supply and demand will determine the bulk of price action.

However, there are additional factors that determine pricing in financial markets. The main factor is psychological. By "psychological" we mean what investors believe may or may not happen. For instance, if investors feel that a specific company is undervalued, they will flock to buy it up. As such, their desire to own this company's stock will cause the price to go up. By the same token, if investors feel there is something wrong with a company, its stock price will plummet.

Also, economic conditions may lead investors to think twice about buying and/or selling. For example, during a recession, investors may be far more cautious. After all, they might be concerned about the long-term effects of the current economic outlook.

Furthermore, company financials, management, and competition play a significant role in its stock valuation. If a company has solid financials, reputable management, and is at the top of its industry, then you have a winner. However, don't be surprised to hear an investor bet on long shots. These are companies that are unproven, or might be poised for a turnaround after a tough spell. However, always be careful with betting on long shots. There is never any guarantee they will play out.

Looking to the Future

To look into the future, you need to look into the past. With stock prices, you can glean into the future by looking at the history of price action. Individual companies all have historical data on the behavior of its market valuation. This information allows you to look toward the future. From its past trend, you can figure out what might happen. Of course, nothing is certain. Still, you may be able to get a good picture of the future.

Therefore, you must become familiar with charts and graphs. These elements are the graphic representation of the data pertaining to price action. The most common graph is a line graph. Line graphs are perfect at showing the behavior of a stock's trend. Moreover, it will enable you to get a sense of what will happen by its patterns.

The study of quantitative data is called "technical analysis." Technical analysis is crucial to making informed decisions. If you make investment decisions based on your subjective appreciation, then you are basically guessing. As such, you must have objective data to make reasonable assumptions on a stock. Otherwise, the risk of losing on a deal grows exponentially.

Market Organization

When you hear about the "stock market," what you are really hearing about is the collection of stock exchanges located throughout the world. A stock exchange is a physical location in which buyers and sellers of financial assets come together. The most famous stock exchange in the world is the New York Stock Exchange located on Wall Street in New York City. This is the place where the bulk of the transactions happen in the United States. Nevertheless, there are similar exchanges in Philadelphia, Chicago, and Miami.

Additionally, there are a number of stock exchanges around the world. Some of the largest are located in European cities such as London, Paris, Frankfurt, and Madrid. In Asia, the most predominant stock exchanges can be found in Shanghai, Tokyo, and Seoul. There are other markets in Latin America, as well.

When you buy and sell stocks, among other assets, you trade directly in one of these stock exchanges. As a result, you must become familiar with the various kinds of assets trade in them. Please keep in mind that you won't always find the same assets in all markets. Some markets specialize in one type of asset over another. Moreover, companies are listed on a single exchange. Thus, a company that is listed in the United States cannot be listed in another country. So, if you are keen on trading specific companies, you might have to look at an overseas market, as well.

Asset Classes

Stocks are not the only assets that are traded in financial markets. There are a plethora of assets to choose from. In this book, we're focusing on stocks. Nevertheless, here is a list of the assets you can trade in financial markets:

- Government bonds (both US and other countries)
- Commodities (agricultural products, cattle, precious metals, industrial metals, energy)
- Currencies (any currency in the world)
- Derivatives (futures, swaps, options)
- Funds (mutual, index, exchange-traded)

These asset classes have a number of instruments you can buy and sell. Some are great for a "buy and hold" strategy, like bonds, while others are better for short-term investments such as commodities. Ultimately, you can choose to invest in any of these asset classes based on your expectations and your goals.

We recommend starting out with stock. It is the best way to get started before branching out into other asset classes. Since some transactions require a greater amount of experience and study, it is important to master stock trading before taking the plunge into other asset classes. Still, you can build a diversified portfolio by investing in various asset classes. Diversification is a great strategy especially when you are looking to protect yourself against long-term risk.

Chapter 3: How to Create an Investment Timeline

Creating an investment timeline is all about managing your expectations. When you are keenly aware of the potential in the market, it is easy to get caught up in the excitement. Many investors engage in wishful thinking. They believe they can score a huge deal that will solve all of their problems.

This is something that you'd only see in the movies.

While it is possible to knock one out of the park, doing so requires time and research. If you can spot a deal like this, you might be poised to clean up. Otherwise, you may find yourself searching for the elusive "big one."

Managing Expectations

The most important part of managing expectations is being realistic. By "realistic" we mean understanding that it takes time to build a winning strategy. Therefore, you need to have patience in the early going. For instance, a realistic assumption would be to make a few hundred dollars in your first month of trading. It may not be enough to pay for all of your expenses, but it would be a welcome windfall.

It is practically impossible to indicate a specific sum of money you could make in your first few weeks of trading. Depending on your strategy and starting capital, you could make anywhere from $200 to $300, to several thousand. However, it's also important to keep in mind that most investors lose money at first. By sticking to their game plan, they turn things around and make up lost ground.

Based on this, it is reasonable to assume that you will make enough money to supplement your monthly income in the early going. If you start with an investment capital such as a few hundred dollars, you might be able to turn that into $100 or more.

Here is a reasonable way of determining how much you could make based on your starting capital. Average market returns range between 5% to 10% annually. If you break it down, that's roughly 1% to 2% a month. That might not seem like a lot. But when you multiply it over the number of transactions and investment capital, you could potentially make a fair amount of money. Later on, we'll discuss the strategies that you can use to maximize your returns.

Most investors reach complete financial independence at different points in their lives. The easy answer is this: the simpler your lifestyle, the sooner you can become financially independent. Consequently, if you only need $1,500 a month to finance your lifestyle, you may get there in a couple of years, if not much sooner. In contrast, if you need $5,000 a month to fund your living expenses, then it might take you several years to get there. In the end, it all boils down to your overall lifestyle.

Determine the Lifestyle You Want

Speaking of lifestyles, having a clear idea of what your ideal lifestyle is, constitutes the backbone of your investment timeline. There is nothing wrong with dreaming big. However, it's important for you to know that financial independence is about financing your lifestyle without the need to work for an indefinite time frame. For some, "indefinite" might mean the rest of their lives. For others, it might just mean taking off as much time as they want.

To calculate how much money you need to finance your lifestyle, all you need is to crunch the numbers. Take your current lifestyle. Use it as a baseline. Add up all of your expenses in a month. Try your best to include everything you spend on. The greater the detail, the more accurate the number.

Now, let's assume your monthly number is $1,000. Thus, you would need to produce an income of $1,000 per month to finance your lifestyle. This is your baseline.

The next step is to figure out the lifestyle that you want. To calculate this number, you would need to figure out how much it would cost you to finance this type of life. You would need to add up all the expenses that would be involved and then come up with a number. So, let's assume that your ideal lifestyle would cost you $2,000. Hence, you would need to first produce $1,000 to achieve financial independence, but then produce $2,000 to get to your ideal lifestyle.

Calculating Financial Independence

To calculate how long it will take you to be financially independent is about consistently hitting the number you need to finance your lifestyle. When you can consistently make enough money to finance your lifestyle, you know you're there. So, if you are able to produce $1,000 (according to our example) for three consecutive months, then you know you have hit the mark.

Let's assume a 5% monthly return rate on your investment. So, to produce $1,000 in profits, you would need to invest $20,000 each month. A 5% return on $20,000 is $1,000. If you have $20,000 on hand at the moment, then generating this type of return will take you a couple of months. But if you are starting out with $1,000, then it will take you several months to achieve this type of return.

To come up with a fairly accurate number, let's take a 5% return on $1,000. That's $50. Next, roll over your profits plus investment capital. So, in month number two, you would invest $1,050. At a 5% return, month number two would yield $52.50. On month number three, you would invest $1,102.50.

In this example, we're using small numbers and assuming very conservative returns. Nevertheless, it illustrates the type of calculation you would need to make to reach your desired target. The main thing to keep in mind here is to resist the temptation to take out your profits during the first few months. If you can simply keep rolling over your investments every month, you'll build up your investment capital. Before you know it, you'll have a large capital to work with. This will make reaching your desired target much easier.

Chapter 4: How to Define Your Investment Strategy

Having an investment strategy is a fundamental aspect of successful stock market trading. Without it, you're essentially groping in the dark. While you may be very adept at technical analysis, you will find it hard to have a clear direction for your portfolio. Of course, you can still make money. However, you won't make the best return you could make.

It is important for you to determine what your game plan is going to be. When you have this plan worked out, you can then go about finding the stocks to match your aims. In this chapter, we are going to look at three great investment strategies you can use to make serious gains.

Buy and Hold

The "buy and hold" strategy is a long-term strategy. In this strategy, you buy up assets and hold on to them until their price shoots up. At that point, you can sell your holdings. Now, it should be noted that the definition of "long term" in stock trading is any time frame over a month. As such, you should expect to hold on to stocks for at least a month.

This strategy is great when you find undervalued stocks. For instance, companies that have great track records but have fallen on hard times. Oil companies are a great example of this. Oil companies have no fault in geopolitical issues that cause the price of oil to fall. Nevertheless, when the price of oil plummets, oil companies take serious hits.

To capitalize on this phenomenon, you buy up oil stocks when they sink. Then, you hold on to them until the price of oil rebounds. Thus, oil stocks rebound as well. In some cases, it might be a question of days. In other cases, it might be a question of weeks. Ultimately, you need to be on top of news and developments across various industries.

High-Frequency Trading

High-frequency trading, or HFT, is a staple of day traders. This is a very short-term strategy. It consists of making multiple trades over and over. You don't make a lot of money per trade with this strategy. However, when you multiply your gains over a large number of transactions, the profits add up.

To make this strategy work, you need to find a stock that is trading in a range. This means that they go up to a specific value and then back down to a certain value. Meanwhile, they don't typically deviate from these limits. As a result, you can fairly predict where the price action will be.

Many times, HFT traders make pennies per trade. But when the total number of trades is calculated, the results could add up to hundreds of dollars a day. Therefore, it is a good strategy to use while you execute the "buy and hold" with other stocks.

Also, HFT is great for investors who are starting with very little investment capital. As such, HFT traders move the same investment capital over and over again. For instance, the invest $1,000 over and over making profits on the same amount of money. In the end, they generate returns is if they had invested $100,000.

As a novice investor, you ought to consider HFT. It will require you to spend some time at your computer setting up deals. But once you get the hang of it, you can easily set everything up at the start of your day, and then sit back to take in all the action.

Value Investing

Value investing consists of finding undervalued stocks and holding them until they bounce back. Now, the main difference between value investing and the buy and hold strategy is that value investing looks to find companies that will rebound in a shorter time frame. In the case of the buy and hold, you are looking to hold stocks for over a month. In value investing, you're looking to hold stocks for days or a couple of weeks.

The trick to value investing is finding stocks that are poised to make a comeback sooner rather than later. To execute the value investing strategy, you need to look at a company's book value. The term "book value" refers to a company's share price based on its accounting. As such, a company's financials will tell you what their share price is really worth. Then, you must compare the company's book value with its market valuation. If you find that the company's market valuation is below its book value, then you have an undervalued company.

However, there is a catch.

When going about value investing, you must ensure that the company is not in serious trouble. Therefore, you need to do your homework carefully. In some cases, a company may be going through a temporary situation. This is not a reflection of poor management or bad financials. As such, you can assume the company will bounce back.

In value investing, things can happen very quickly. So, you need to be ready for the possible changes that may take place. Still, it is a very good strategy when you're looking for an intermediate step between the buy and hold and HFT.

Setting Objectives

The strategies mentioned in this chapter are all aligned to your objectives. Whether you're looking to supplement your monthly income or become a billionaire, you need to be clear on what you want to achieve. Then, you can align your strategy.

Generally speaking, novice investors start with HFT, then move up to value investing before using the buy and hold. Ultimately, you can combine all three strategies to keep your portfolio engaged in the short, medium, and long term. As such, you will gain exposure to all investment time frames.

This approach will help you make short-term gains while allowing you to cash in on the big trades that happen in the long term. This is the reason why it is so important for you to do your homework. Thus, the more informed you are, the easier it will be for you to make some serious returns.

Chapter 5: Fundamentals of Day Trading

To invest in stocks, you can go the usual route. So, you can buy mutual funds or pay a stockbroker to manage your portfolio. However, this route will only get you so far. You'll be quite surprised to find the potential returns to be quite underwhelming.

Because of underwhelming returns, many investors choose to go at it alone. This is the reason why they turn to day trading. In this chapter, we'll be looking at the fundamentals of day trading, and why it might be a good choice for you.

Definition of Day Trading

Day trading is a stock investing approach in which the investor takes full control of their portfolio. In other words, the investor decides what stocks to buy and sell. Moreover, the investor decides when to make trades happen.

By definition, day trading is a short-term trading approach. Investors open and close positions on the same trading day. Therefore, they start and end the day with a clean slate. The reason for this is simplicity. If you leave positions open overnight, you might become vulnerable to external factors. The result may be unexpected shifts in price action.

Therefore, investors seek to avoid becoming vulnerable by closing all of their positions at the end of the trading. As such, they cash out for the day. This is a highly practical approach as it enables investors to avoid dealing with possible price shocks that may occur at the start of the trading day.

Day trading is perfect for those investors who are starting out with relatively small investment capital and are looking to make short-term gains. For those investors with larger investment capital, day trading may be one part of their overall investment approach.

How to Get Started With Day Trading

To get started with day trading, you need a brokerage account. A brokerage account is an agreement that you enter with a financial institution. This institution is a duly license stock trading corporation. Hence, this corporation allows you to gain access to the market through the use of their trading platform. In short, you become a stockbroker yourself. The only downside is that you are solely responsible for anything that happens. So, if you lose all your money, you have no one to blame but yourself.

There are two main types of brokerage accounts. There is a "full service" account. This account type gives you all the bells and whistles. These accounts charge a sign-up fee in addition to transaction fees per trade. Yet, they provide you with real-time quotes and analytics. Also, they provide expert advice and recommendations. Thus, they facilitate the process of deciding where to allocate your funds.

The other type of account is a "discount" account. When you sign up with a discount broker, you mainly receive access to the trading platform but without the bells and whistles. Therefore, you need to figure out where you can get information on the stocks you wish to trade. The good thing about discount brokers is that they charge a one-time sign-up fee. They also have lower transaction fees per trade. Although, you would need to buy trade bundles as opposed to a pay-as-you-go strategy.

Once you sign up for a brokerage account, you are ready to trade. It is relatively straightforward. However, do keep in mind that brokerage accounts vary in conditions. Some may require you to have several thousand dollars' worth of investment capital while others may only require you to have as little as $500.

One very important thing to keep in mind is the free demo account. Any reputable brokerage firm will grant you free access to the platform via a demo account. In a demo account, you play the real game using monopoly money. As such, you are trading on the real platform, with real data and analytics, but not with real money. This is why a demo account is great. It allows you to test out your strategy before you go live with real trades. It affords you the opportunity to make mistakes without losing your shirt in the process.

The Best Day Trading Strategy

The best day trading strategy, especially for beginners, is HFT. HFT is quite easy to master. That is why HFT is the best strategy for new investors. Plus, it doesn't require a great deal of investment capital. If you sign up for a discount account, you can turn $500 into a fairly decent amount in a few weeks. Naturally, the more trades you make, the greater your chances of making your capital grow.

Early on, you ought to consider rolling over your profits. It is recommended that you resist the temptation of pulling out your winnings. The idea is to build up your investment capital so that it can produce even greater returns.

The only catch to HFT is transaction fees. Please make sure that you are perfectly aware of how much your broker charges per trade. It could be that high transaction fees zap your profits. To avoid getting hit with high transaction fees, it's a good idea to purchase bundles. For example, your broker may offer 10 trades for $2.99. This type of package allows you to calculate your cost, thereby enabling you to visualize your returns.

How to Determine if Day Trading Is for You

Naturally, day trading is not for everyone. To be successful, day trading requires a commitment to learning the trading platform. By learning the platform, you'll be able to set up all your deals appropriately. Then, you can let the platform do its job.

Day trading may not be right for you if you are looking to become a passive investor. As a passive investor, you are not keen on becoming actively involved in trading. Nevertheless, day trading can help you become a passive investor as it would only require you to go about setting up your deals at the outset of the trading day. By the end of the day, the system will close out your positions. Meanwhile, you can spend your time researching your next move.

Chapter 6: How to Succeed at Day Trading

When you go about day trading, it is essential to have strategies that you can use to help you make money most of the time. If you lack reliable go-to strategies, you may find yourself guessing about what to do. Thus, having a clear idea of what you can do at all times is the best way to get ahead in the game.

In this chapter, we are going to take a look at some core strategies to help you make money while also helping you get ahead of the game. Now, it's worth noting that most investors have a 50% to 60% success rate. In general, investors win most trades. However, please be prepared to lose. So, your strategy boils down to what you can do when things don't work out. Your reaction in these situations will enable you to become a highly successful investor.

Core Strategies

To be successful, you must follow these core strategies. They are cross-cutting recommendations that you can implement any time you choose to enter a trade. Moreover, these strategies are time-tested tactics that can keep you safe from the mistake novice investors make. Therefore, do keep them at the forefront of your mind as you engage in stock investing.

Money management

Money management refers to the way you manage your investment capital. This is an approach that you can use to help you develop discipline in your asset allocation. There are two main rules that you need to follow.

- **The golden rule**. This rule refers to limiting the amount of capital you sink into individual trades. The golden rule states that you must never invest more than 2% of your total investment capital into a single trade. While you can invest the full sum of your capital, you shouldn't invest it all in a single trade. Please keep in mind that the more money you sink into an individual trade, the greater the risk.

- **Doubling down**. When investors lose money, they are tempted to invest twice as much in the next trade to compensate for the loss in the previous one. This strategy is highly dangerous. It can lead you to lose twice as much as you did before. For example, if you lost $100 on a trade, you might be tempted to invest $200 in the one. However, if something goes wrong, you risk losing $200 on top of the original $100. So, it's best to simply follow your strategy. You'll eventually recoup your losses.

Timing the market

Generally speaking, the largest amount of trading activity happens at the beginning and end of the trading session. Therefore, these are the times when you need to jump into the fray. The first two hours of the trading day show a flurry of activity. Here, you can perfectly implement an HFT strategy. You can make multiple trades within a short two-hour window. Some traders open and close positions in a matter of seconds. The same goes for the last hour and a half prior to market closing. This is a perfect time to liquidate any open positions. However, you need to be careful as the market selloff right before the end of the day may cause you to take a cut on your profits.

Time Management

Time management is about being consistent. Investing time daily to develop your craft is ideal. If you only go over charts or look at your trading platform once or twice a week, you may be surprised to find that your results aren't what you expect them to be. As a result, being consistent in the amount of time you spend is key.

Most successful day traders spend about two to three hours a day on their trading platform in addition to any time they spend on research. If you have a full-service account, much of the research is done for you. So, all you have to do is go over your news feed to see where you want to place your trades. You can then set up the system to take care of everything for you.

Core Components

Every good strategy regardless of its structure must have the following three components. These components are always present. Therefore, you cannot ignore them. If you fail to acknowledge them, they'll come back to bite you. So, it's best to take care of them right away. Doing so will help you avoid a myriad of problems later on.

Liquidity

Liquidity refers to the ease you would have to buy and sell an asset. Some assets are highly liquid while others are not. This term refers to how easily you could sell something especially in times of turmoil. For example, a house is a great example of an illiquid asset. After all, you can't expect to sell a house in five minutes. It may take weeks, even months, before you get a good offer.

Highly liquid assets include desirable stocks (blue-chip companies like Apple, Facebook, or GM), commodities (gold, oil), or currencies. Depending on the nature of the asset, you may have offers already lined up. So, make sure to focus on liquid assets.

In contrast, illiquid assets may be highly profitable but hard to move during a market downturn. For instance, real estate, intellectual property, or industrial assets are all valuable but hard to find buyers. These assets are much better for a buy and hold strategy as opposed to a short-term one.

Volatility

Volatility refers to the amount of trading volume occurring at any point. For example, volatility picks up at the beginning of the trading day. This is a natural occurrence derived from the entry of all players into the game.

Volatility can also increase when there are unexpected events in the economy. These events can come in the form of government policy, natural disasters, or poor economic data. However, these events may also be positive. If they are positive events, volatility may pick up in terms of buying rather than selling.

When volatility is low, you may not have the chance to make significant gains. Therefore, an HFT approach is best. If volatility is high, you might find that undervalued companies may rise to the occasion. So, it's best to find undervalued companies before volatility picks up. Then, when volatility rises, you can sell amid the frenzy.

Volume

Volume refers to the number of times an individual has been traded during a specific time frame. Volume in an indication of how liquid a stock is. As such, the lower the volume, the less popular the stock is. Therefore, you might have trouble selling it in a short time window. In contrast, if a stock has a high trading volume, then you can confidently but it and sell it whenever you need to. This is the core indicator you need to look at when considering an individual stock for HFT.

Most Successful Day Trading Strategies

Let's take a look at the most successful day trading strategies. These strategies can help you make a great deal of money when executed correctly. In some cases, you can hit it out of the park. Please note that these strategies are not always suited for HFT. So, you may have to hold on to stocks for a few hours as opposed to a few minutes. Nevertheless, the profits can make up the difference.

1. **Breakout**

This strategy refers to stock breaking past a specific upper limit. A stock's upper limit is known as a "resistance level." This is a psychological barrier in which investors are unwilling to surpass. In other words, investors feel that this point makes the stock too expensive. However, there are times in which investors are waiting for an event before deciding to buy up the stock. For example, investors may be waiting for economic data from the government. If the data is positive, they jump in. If the data is bad, they will hold.

Entry point: To determine your entry point in this trade, take a look at the stock's price history. If you find that it was at a higher price point previously, you have a reference to where the price could land. The stock is poised to break out when you see its price hit the resistance level but not surpass it. After three successive hits on a resistance level, the stock may be ready to achieve a breakthrough. While the timing is unpredictable, indications are that it will happen very quickly. So, do keep this in mind.

Exit point: The exit point of your trade is any point above the resistance level. A good rule of thumb is to place your sell price at a reasonable level. For example, anything close to or at its previous high is a good idea. Unless there is reason to believe that the price will break past its previous highs, you are better off sticking to its previous high. Depending on your entry point, you could really make a killing.

2. **Reversal**

A reversal is when a stock's price is trending downward, levels off, and the rises. The opposite is also true. Therefore, reversals are highly useful as both entry and exit points. To execute this strategy, you need to be aware of the stock's price history. Based on this, you can determine if and when a reversal in trend will take place.

Let's consider a downward trend. This is also called a "bearish" trend. When there is a bearish trend, a stock's price will eventually fall to a specific point and then rebound. It can be quite difficult to predict the exact point in which it will happen. But with the use of technical analysis, you can spot the point in which trend is about to reverse.

To spot the reversal, you must look at the point in which the trendline stops falling and then flattens out. Then, you can see the point in which the trendline will begin to rise. Sometimes, the trendline will have a "V" shape. This means it falls, hits a point, and then bounces back up immediately. The point right before the price begins to rebound is your optimal entry point. Therefore, this is the lowest price you can buy before the stock begins to rise.

In the opposite scenario, you have a "bullish" trend. This type of trend means the price is rising to a point in which it will come back down. The point right before the price drops back down is your optimal sell point. As such, this is the point where you'll make the most profit.

When you use reversals, you can buy at the lowest possible point and then sell at the highest possible price. This is how you can maximize profits.

3. Momentum or piggybacking

In this strategy, you are "riding the wave." It is best executed when there is news that alters investors' perceptions. For example, a company announces better-than-expected earnings. So, as soon as you hear the news, you buy it. As the wave rises, you sell. This will help you make some quick profits. However, you need to be careful not to wait too long. In this strategy, investors want to rise to the highest part of the wave. The problem is that waiting too long may set you up for a precipitous crash. In the best of cases, you'd see your profits reduced. In the worst of cases, you might end up losing money on the deal. Therefore, piggybacking is about entering quickly, making a profit, and then pulling out. It is a very short-term strategy. Thus, you must be ready to act quickly. Riding on momentum is relatively predictable especially during earnings season. It's a perfect way to make some quick funds during moments of increased volatility and volume.

The same can also be done when a stock pulls back. Often, stocks drop in price right before rising. This is commonly referred to as "buying on the dip." This strategy allows for short-term gains especially when there is a high degree of volatility. So, keep your eyes open for these movements. They can prove to be quite profitable in the short term.

Chapter 7: Fundamentals of Swing Trading

Swing trading is another approach investors use to maximize profits. This approach calls for more patience as investors are looking toward a longer time frame. As such, swing trading goes beyond the one-day time frame of day trading. With swing trading, investors hold open positions for periods ranging from a few days to several weeks.

The main purpose of swing trading is to capitalize on market "swings." Since we're looking at a longer time frame, we're anticipating much larger swings in price action. Instead of focusing on price action that shifts in pennies, we're anticipating much larger swings. Depending on the size of a position, this could represent hundreds, if not thousands of dollars.

Difference Between Day and Swing Trading

On the whole, day and swing trading work in the same way. The same type of trading platform is used. Also, the same techniques and analytical tools are used. The main difference lies in the time frame in which trades are placed. Day trading calls for opening and closing positions within the same trading session. In swing trading, you need to be prepared to keep your positions open for a much longer time frame. However, this is how you maximize profit.

Another important difference lies in the use of risk/reward ratios. In essence, a risk/reward ratio is based upon a potential loss versus a potential gain. Naturally, if the gain outweighs the loss, then the deal is worth entering. For instance, a good rule of thumb is a 3:1 risk to reward ratio. In other words, you stand to make $3 while risking a loss of $1.

In the case of day trading, risk to reward ratios doesn't make much sense as the trade is so short-term.

It's also worth mentioning that swing trading requires patience. You need to be willing to sit and wait for market swings to occur. They are highly unpredictable. Therefore, you need to ready to wait until you reach your desired price points. Otherwise, you may exit the trade before achieving your desired price point.

Use Technical Analysis and Fundamental Analysis

Technical analysis is the use of quantitative tools to analyze price action information. Here, we're talking about price, volatility, and volume. These indicators provide objective data you can use to base your decisions. As a result, you're not basing your investment choices on hunches.

Fundamental analysis is the study of non-quantitative factors that influence price action. These are mainly economic, political, and most importantly, psychological factors. Fundamental analysis is essential when looking at a long-term picture. For example, political decisions by the government influence investors' mindset. Consequently, when investors become uneasy about potential shifts in the market, they may choose to sit on the sidelines. By the same token, if the outlook is positive, you may find investors jumping into the fray. Therefore, a close study of fundamental analysis is essential in any successful swing trading strategy.

To be successful at swing trading, you need to become familiar with both technical analysis and fundamental analysis. Therefore, swing trading requires a greater commitment in terms of time and effort. You need to pay close attention to market conditions. This will enable you to foresee opportunities. When you get really good at spotting future swings, you can make considerable profits.

Advantages of Swing Trading

Let's take a look at the advantages that come with swing trading.

1. **Swing trading requires less time than day trading**

Even though you need a greater commitment of time and effort in conducting research, the overall amount of time required to engage in swing trading is much less. The reason for this lies in the time it takes to set up trades. In day trading, you need to be at your computer every day, setting up trades, and monitoring your positions.

In the case of swing trading, you set up trades with a longer time frame. Therefore, you won't be placing nearly as many trades. If you plan on doing a combination of day and swing trading, you would still be making fewer trades. Thus, you could conceivably set up trades, and go for days without touching any of your positions. In the meantime, you would be free to continue your research.

2. **Profit maximization**

You stand to make much more profits as you ride large waves as opposed to short-term times. These large waves are the result of capturing significant swings in the market. By spotting these potential swings early on, you can set yourself up for massive gains.

3. **Decisions are based on technical analysis**

In swing trading, technical analysis will tell you what you can expect. While there is certainly a place for hunches, you must base all of your decisions on technical analysis. As such, you'll be able to spot reversals in trend, changes in trading volume, or the emergence of resistance and support levels. Therefore, you need to pay close attention to the fundamentals of technical analysis.

Disadvantages of Swing Trading

Now, let's take a look at the disadvantages that come with swing trading.

1. **You are vulnerable to risk**

Since you have open positions for longer time frames, you are open to greater risk, particularly with overnight markets. Since developments can occur at any time, you might wake up one morning to a drastically different landscape. Thus, the use of stop-loss triggers is vital to ensuring you don't get wiped out in a single trade.

2. **Sudden market reversals**

Since markets are relatively unpredictable, any sudden changes can expose you to significant risk. As such, you need to ensure that you are aware of the potential risks. This situation implies that you must use stop-loss or take-profit triggers to ensure that you capture your desired price points.

3. **Short-term trends outweigh long-term ones**

Even though swing trading has a longer time frame than day trading, it's still a short-term approach. As such, swing traders are more focused on short-term profits rather than long-term ones. This is a necessary approach as swing traders are looking to make as much money as possible in the least amount of time. Since there is no telling what can happen, it's best to cash out as soon as your desired price points are hit.

Are you enjoying this book? If so, i'd be really happy if you could leave a short review on Amazon, it means a lot to me! Thank you!

Chapter 8: How to Succeed at Swing Trading

To be successful at swing trading, you need to become highly familiar with technical analysis. This will be the cornerstone of your strategy. Thus, you must do your homework by consistently checking in on price charts. Based on your observation and analysis, you'll be able to determine what stocks are ripe for the plucking.

However, you don't need to have a crystal ball to figure everything on your own. Lots of investors rely on experts' advice and analysis. You hear these pundits on television or read their columns. They can provide you with insight and knowledge that you may not have been familiar with. As such, it's always good to listen. Nevertheless, always take what they say with a grain of salt.

Mainly, it's important for you to take everything you hear and read and verify the information with your analysis. As a result, you can contrast the opinions you get from the media. Additionally, analytics services like Bloomberg or Market Watch provide an expert recommendation. These analyses are generally available to subscribers only. So, you might want to consider purchasing a subscription. While it is not necessary for you to purchase one, you might want to consider it anyway. The best course of action would be a free trial. That way, you can see if the information is worth the money you would be paying for it.

Swing Trading Strategies

Swing trading strategies require you to dig deeper into the history and trend of price action. This is important as historical data will help you glean into the patterns the stock is trading. When you learn to spot these patterns, you can anticipate what will happen with reasonable accuracy. Anyone who masters technical analysis can predict what will happen. The only thing you need to be aware of is that predict time is nearly impossible. Of course, ballpark estimations are certainly reasonable. However, it's virtually impossible to determine the date and time market shifts will take place. Therefore, you must think twice before believing anyone who claims they can "time" the market.

To make the most of the strategies we will describe herein, please take the time to go over historical data. Most financial news services will provide you with historical data on stock prices. Many will go back at least 10 years. Although, you would only need two or three years' worth of data at most. Going back this far will allow you to determine patterns and trends in stock prices. From there, you will find patterns emerging.

To establish these patterns, you must become familiar with an indicator known as the "moving average."

Moving Average

The moving average is an indicator that is calculated based on historical data. In short, a moving average is the average between the buy and sell price in a given time frame. Depending on the chart, this could be presented on an hourly or daily basis. Some highly specialized real-time charts may present moving average information on a minute-by-minute basis. However, this is not as common as reading hourly data.

Investors and traders use the moving average as a means of determining the overall trend in the price of a stock. Thus, there are three possible types of trends: bearish, bullish, and flat.

A bullish trend means that the price of the stock is rising. While you will find that that chart reflects ups and downs in the overall price action of a stock, the trendline indicates that the price of the stock is rising. Therefore, you can consider this is a bullish trend. Now, it might be impossible to determine how high the price will go. To get an idea, look at previous highs. That should give you an indication of how high the price can go. Unless the stock is experiencing a breakout, you can expect it to fall somewhere around its previous high.

A bearish trend is the opposite of a bullish one. In a bearish trend, the moving average indicates that the price is falling. Hence, you can use this information to either plan an entry point, or stay away from the stock until its price action settles down. Bearish trends usually emerge when the overall trend in the market is down. Nevertheless, individual stocks may fall even though the overall trend in the market is bullish.

A flat or sideways trend means there is no clearly defined trend. As such, it is neither bearish nor bullish. This situation generally indicates that investors are sitting on their hands. In other words, investors are looking to avoid entering the market or selling their positions. This reaction, or lack thereof, is the result of an uncertain situation. When investors don't know what to expect, they may delay making trades as long as possible. To capitalize on a sideways trend, you need to look at the trend leading up to the sideways action. For example, if the trend was bullish, but then it leveled off, you might expect a sharp downturn. In contrast, if the trend was bearish and the leveled off, you might expect a reversal into a bullish one. Unless you have a reasonable belief that the previous trend will continue, the likeliest scenario is that prices will eventually reverse.

10-Day and 20-Day Simple Moving Average

A great tactic swing traders use is called the "simple moving average." This tactic is used as a means of calculating the average daily price of a stock by "smoothing" it out. The term "smoothing" is used in statistics to refer to the process of eliminating fluctuations from a data set. When fluctuations are eliminated, it is possible to see where the overall trend of the data set lies.

To do this, two separate measures are used the 10-day and the 20-day simple moving average. The reason for using these measures lies in using historical data to predict future short-term shifts. Thus, if you want to look at long-term shifts, then you need to look at long-term data such as the 50-day and 200-day moving average.

To produce the simple moving average indicator, all you need to do is add up the average price of the last ten days. After adding them up, divide them by 10. This will give you the average price of the last 10 days. Now, take two separate sets, that is 20 days, and add them together. If you find a divergence between the two indicators, then you have a signal.

A buy signal is sent when the 10-day simple moving average is greater than the 20-day one. This indicates that the price is rising. In contrast, if the 10-day simple moving average is lower than the 20-day one, you must sell. This indicates that the price is heading downward.

You can use this tactic as a means of determining your entry and exits points. Let's assume you don't hold any position. You spot the buy signal, so you set your entry point. Then, you hold until you see the next 10-day moving average cross the 20-day. Once you get the sign to sell, you immediately liquidate your position.

Now, does this mean you have to wait another 10 days before you sell?

No, you don't have to. What you do is you calculate the 10-day moving average every day. All you do is eliminate the 10th day and add the last day. This is why it's called a "moving" average. By doing this, you can spot the exact point in which the price action flashes either a "sell" or "buy" signal.

Moving Average Convergence Divergence Crossover

The moving average convergence divergence (MACD) is commonly used in swing trading to help investors pinpoint when to buy or sell. Unlike the simple moving average, the MACD flashes signals based on two lines, the moving average line (trendline) and the signal line. Most charts represent these are red and blue. Although, you might find any number of color combinations.

The MACD is automatically generated by most stock tracking charts. Also, they are generally available for free. So, you don't need to get an expensive subscription package to have access to these indicators. To take advantage of these indicators, you need to pay attention to the points in which the lines cross one another. This is called a "crossover." Depending on the trend, this will indicate a sell or buy signal.

For instance, when the MACD line crosses over (higher) the signal line, then this indicates the trend is bullish. Therefore, it is a signal to buy. You can also determine this visually as the lines themselves are moving upward. When the MACD line crosses belove (lower) the signal line, then this is a sell line as you can anticipate a bearish trend. Of course, this signal can also be an indication of a "buy" signal if you don't hold an open position. All you have to do is keep an eye on the lines right before the intersect again. This is the lowest price you could buy.

It is important to keep in mind that if you sell after the MACD cross over occurs at the top of the trendline, then you would have missed out on the highest possible returns. Hence, you need to sell right before the lines intersect. This will provide you with the highest possible returns.

Breakout Strategy

The breakout strategy is when you anticipate the price of a stock to blow past its previous highs. To make this strategy work, you need to use the 10-day average to keep a close eye on the stock's overall trend.

Here's how it works.

1. First, identify the trend in the stock of your choice. The trend must be a bullish one. A stock with a bearish trend will not work in this case. If anything, a stock with a bearish trend may break through its floor.

2. Second, look for a double top or triple top pattern. This pattern consists of two or three successive hits upon the stock's upper limit. You must spot at least two hits. If you spot three consecutive hits, then the breakout is imminent.

3. Third, set up your trade. Generally speaking, there is no telling how high the breakout will go. So, it's best to play it safe. You may find that the stock pulls back before continuing to rise. Consequently, you must strive to sell before the pullback. You can always sell, then buy on the pullback, and sell on the new rise.

4. Lastly, cash out as soon as you see your price point hit. It doesn't matter if the stock continues to rise. It's best to liquate your position before the pullback. Otherwise, your profits may be reduced completely.

With the breakout strategy, you must be aware of the resistance level in the stock. In general, the breakout is imminent when the trading volume dries up. This means that very few trades are being placed compared to the previous volume. The reason for this is generally due to investors expecting a specific action. For example, this action may be government data or some other event.

The most important thing to watch for is greed. Please avoid overriding your take-profit points. There is no telling when the stock's price might pull back. When this happens, the stock may regress before taking off again. Thus, you need to sell before the pullback and then re-enter your position when the stock pulls back. That way, you can capture the new rise.

On the whole, the breakout strategy is the most successful strategy that investors use to make substantial profits. If you can capture a stock at its lowest point, and then ride the wave all the way past the breakout, you are in great shape to make substantial gains. This is the reason why swing trading is all about making patience and timing. Additionally, you must become familiar with technical analysis. Otherwise, it will be very difficult for you to capture the positive swings in the market.

Chapter 9: Fundamentals of Position Trading

Position trading is the longest-term approach in stock trading. This is where investors are willing to lay their money down for a longer time frame in hopes of capturing significant shifts in the market or individual stocks. As a result, position traders don't really care too much about the ups and downs of day-to-day trading. They are more concerned about the big picture. Consequently, position traders are far likelier to look at trades happening in terms of weeks and months rather than days.

It's worth noting that position traders are not passive investors. Passive investors are the ones who employ the "buy and hold" strategy. As such, passive investors simply put their money into an investment and wait for the return at some point. In contrast, position investors are focused on the trend. This approach implies that the trend will lead to the investor's ultimate goal. Therefore, technical analysis and fundamental analysis play a huge role in determining how a trade will be set up.

Understanding Long-Term Trend

In stock trading, any time frame that surpasses a month is considered long-term. In swing trading, it is not surprising to find investors holding their positions for over a month. However, they rarely hold open positions for any period longer than 30 days. Anything after 30 days would fall into the realm of position trading.

The long-term trend is all about identifying where the price of an individual stock may go. This often implies that you need to ride out short-term fluctuations and pullbacks. As a result, you may actually lose value before reaching your ultimate target. This is the reason why position trading is not for investors seeking short-term profits. Position trading is for those who are concerned with truly maximizing their profits.

Typically, position traders aren't overly active. They may place anywhere between 10 to 20 trades per year. However, those trades make should make enough money to offset the time it takes for them to pay off. In the end, position trading provides investors with a lucrative opportunity to cash in on the big picture market shifts.

Advantages of Position Trading

Here are the most significant advantages of position trading

1. **Position trading doesn't demand much time**

Position trading requires upfront planning. However, once the trade is set up, all the investor needs to do is monitor the situation. Once the conditions unfold, the investor can then execute the transaction. Therefore, this trading approach does not require a great deal of time to pursue.

2. **Profit maximization**

Long-term trends generally yield the highest returns. In short-term trading, profit margins can be limited to a few pennies on the dollar. In long-term trading, profits can be several dollars per share. So, when you multiply them over a large number of shares, profits truly add up.

3. **Risk management**

Position trading offers investors the opportunity to manage risk more carefully. In particular, short-term fluctuations are meaningless. Therefore, slight pullbacks are not of concern. As a matter of fact, short-term fluctuations are just a part of the deal. This approach offers greater flexibility. This enables investors to cash out in case they need to leave their position at any time.

Disadvantages of Position Trading

Position trading also has its disadvantages. So, let's take a look at them.

1. **Money is tied up for a long time**

The duration of trades is the biggest disadvantage of position trading. Some investors are not interested in keeping their money tied up for so long. As such, they would much rather engage in shorter-term deals. This enables them to move their money around, thereby generating smaller, but more consistent profits.

2. **There are no guarantees**

While position trading offers the possibility of significant returns, there is no guarantee they will materialize. This situation leads investors to think twice about investing their money for any period beyond three or four weeks. Also, it is worth noting that conditions can change overnight. As a result, investors are always exposed to risk.

3. **Opportunity cost**

The term "opportunity cost" refers to the choice you need to make between one thing or another. In this case, you choose to invest in a stock over another. While this is a common decision investors frequently make, investing over a longer time frame magnifies this situation. For instance, investing in a stock for three months means you can't use those funds to trade other stocks throughout that time frame. Thus, your options suddenly become limited. This is the reason why the profits from position trading need to outweigh short-term profits made through day and swing trading.

Combined Strategy

If you consider using position trading as part of a combined strategy, you can truly make your portfolio go into high gear. Hence, you can use position trading as part of a diversified portfolio. For example, you can be a dedicated day trader looking for consistent, short-term gains. Then, you can use swing trading to capitalize on trend reversals and breakouts. Lastly, you can use position trading to capture larger market shifts, especially when you can't quite pinpoint when these shifts will happen.

The main advantage of having a diversified portfolio lies in ensuring that you capture the various time frames the market has to offer. When you have your portfolio spread out over various strategies, you will find that you can make money on a consistent basis.

As for risk, diversification allows you to manage it more effectively. If you place all of your investment capital in a position trading approach, it will be hard for you to make consistent returns. If you neglect long-term market movements, you may miss out on short-term opportunities. Hence, making use of all timeframes helps you capture the bulk of the market's price action.

Lastly, position trading is a great way to invest money, particularly when you are more focused on the big picture. This big-picture approach gives you the opportunity to correct your strategy on the fly. You can enter and exit trades within a reasonable time frame. With short-term investing, you have to roll with the punches. As a result, position trading gives you a higher degree of flexibility as part of your overall strategy.

Chapter 10: How to Succeed at Position Trading

Being successful in position trading is all about anticipating market movements. Since it's impossible to determine the exact moment in which movements will happen, you need to be ready to capitalize at any time. This is the reason why the position remains open for so long. You don't know when prices will go up or down. Nevertheless, you set up your trades so that you're ready for them.

Since you are looking for trends, the main thing is to be ready for the signals that may indicate a reversal. If you are holding a position, you need to be ready for a possible reversal. In this possible reversal, you will get a signal indicating a sale. If you are looking to enter a trade, then a reversal in a bearing trend will indicate your entry point. This is the core strategy around position trading. The issue here is figuring out at what point you need to enter and exit trades.

Like swing trading, position trading uses the moving average as its main technical analysis tool. The difference is that instead of looking at the 10-day or 20-day moving average, we're going to be looking at the 50-day and 200-day moving average.

50-Day and 200-Day Moving Average

These indicators are exactly like the other indicators we discussed earlier. The difference is the time frame they analyze. Analyzing a longer time frame enables you to see the broader trend in a stock. This will help you determine if the price action you have seen is part of the stock's overall trend or not.

For instance, a stock falls sharply in a span of three trading days. On the surface, this movement indicates the stock is in a bearish trend. However, when you look at the 50-day moving average, you can see the stock is actually up. Therefore, this sharp decline is a pullback.

Now, if you are looking to confirm your observations, then you must look at the 200-day moving average. In this indicator, you can confirm the observations from the 50-day moving average. As such, you can confirm the trend or determine it to be the opposite.

Another common situation is steep increases. A stock may show significant increases over a few trading sessions. Yet, the stock is actually down over the 200-day period. Therefore, you can conclude that it's in a bearish trend. The increase in price may simply be the result of market momentum but not a reflection on this stock's true valuation.

These are the observations that you can make when looking at longer time frames. A day trader would not be concerned with these longer-term trends. A day trader would only be interested in seeing the price action over the shorter time frame. As a result, they could capitalize on the fluctuation in the price over one or two trading sessions. Moreover, a swing trader would bank on the movements occurring over three or four trading sessions without really paying much attention to what occurred prior to that.

In position trading, it is important to keep an eye on the big picture. As long as you keep your eyes on the larger scope of the market, you'll be able to spot the potential to make money. So, you should not neglect the way the markets move in addition to individual stocks. This will provide you with the best chance to make serious returns.

Determining Entry and Exit Points

You can use the 50-day and 200-day moving averages in an MACD crossover pattern. In this case, you execute your entry and exit points based on the trendline and the MACD line. When these lines cross over, you can establish your entry and exit points.

Let's consider a bullish trend. In this situation, you have an open position. As such, you are anticipating a climb in the stock's price. You must look at the overall trend, that 200-day moving average, to determine if there is a bullish or bearish trend. Since the 200-day moving average signals a bullish trend, you must wait for the moment in which both lines intersect. At the point in which the 50-day moving average crosses the 200-day moving average, then you have an exit point. This is the point at which you must sell.

At this point, two things can happen. The first thing is a possible trend reversal. The second is a flattening of the trendline. In either case, you stand to see your profit reduced. Thus, you must liquidate your position as close to the intersection point as possible.

In the case of a bearish trend, the point in which the 50-day intersects the 200-day moving average is your optimal entry point. This is the lowest point the stock will hit before bouncing up. As a result, you stand to make the largest profit. If you get into the trade too soon, the price of your stock will fall even further before it rebounds. This situation may cause you to become impatient. Plus, your profit would not be optimal as you could have bought the stock at a lower point. Consequently, you must try your best to get in at the point closest to the intersection of both moving averages.

Pullback and Retracement Strategy

Pullbacks are temporary dips that stocks experience during a bullish trend. Pullbacks can happen for any number of reasons. As such, it's important to look at the overall picture. When you can clearly spot the overall bullish trends, pullbacks provide great opportunities to pick up shares at a cheaper. While the ideal approach is to get in at the lowest point of the trend, you can still capitalize on pullbacks to augment your position.

Position traders use pullbacks all the time to make shorter-term trades, much like swing trading, to generate some additional income while they wait for the big trade to come through. So, these dips in price can provide you with the opportunity to make some immediate profits particularly when you are looking to ride the overall trend.

A retracement is a type of pullback. It is a temporary dip in the price. The difference is that retracements follow a specific pattern. This pattern allows you to determine where the price will fall. Thus, you can plan the points at which you can place additional trades.

The most popular type of retracement strategy is known at the "Fibonacci" retracement. A Fibonacci retracement is based on the classic Fibonacci sequence. When this sequence is applied to a stock chart, you can determine entry and exit points for your trades. Please bear in mind that the overall trend is not expected to change. As such, you are still expecting to ride the wave all the way to the top. Nevertheless, a Fibonacci retracement provides you with the opportunity to plot your movements more accurately.

Here's how it works.

The Fibonacci retracement strategy is based on the Fibonacci sequence of 1, 2, 3, 5, 8, 13, 21, 34, 55, etc. This sequence is present throughout various elements of nature. When applied to stock trading, it enables you to plot specific price points in a chart. Consequently, you can reasonably assume where a price point may be useful to you.

It may seem incredible that stock market fluctuations act according to a similar pattern as the Fibonacci sequence. This is the reason why the Fibonacci retracement strategy is quite useful. Of course, it's not infallible, but produces a lot of positive results most of the time.

The Fibonacci retracement strategy is calculated by placing six lines on a price chart. To do this, you need to take a price chart over any time frame. For the purpose of position trading, you can use a 50-day or 200-day chart. However, you could use a daily chart with hourly price points if you wanted to.

The first two lines correspond to the 100% and 0% levels. The 100% level corresponds to the highest price point in the chart while the 0% corresponds to the lowest. Based on this, you will now plot the 23.6%, 38.2%, 50%, and 61.8% levels. The 50% level corresponds to the exact middle of the chart. Hence, you would add the highest and lowest prices, and then divide them by two. This would give you the exact middle. The 23.6% and 38.2% would represent potential entry points. The 61.8% would be a good exit point. Some investors also like to plot the 75% level as a reference point.

To calculate your entry points, look at how many times the price points intersected at the 23.6% and 38.2% levels. If you find that the price points intersect several times, then you have potential entry points you can rely on. Then, take a look at the 61.8% level as this would be your likeliest exit point.

If you find that none of the points plotted in the Fibonacci retracement strategy intersects with the actual price points in the chart, then you are better off waiting for the overall trend to hit the mark you are expecting. Generally speaking, this is due to a high degree of volatility. Still, Fibonacci retracements are rarely off the mark. So, they can provide you with great reference points.

Resistance Levels and Breakouts

Whenever you experience a breakout, a new resistance level is set. This means that the price of a stock breaks out of its current resistance level and then settles at a higher price point. Therefore, the floor on the stock elevates while a new, much higher resistance level, is set.

This strategy is great because it allows you to determine where new price points can guide your trades. Consider this situation.

A stock currently trading at $11 a share has a support level of $9 and a resistance level of $12. As such, you expect this price to break past the $12 barrier due to technical and fundamental factors. Sure enough, the price bolts past $12 and hits a new high of $15. At this point, you expect the new resistance level to settle somewhere around the $14 to $15 range. After multiple spikes and pullbacks, there are three consecutive hits on the $14.50 mark. Consequently, you determine this to be the new resistance level.

Now, there is also a new support level. This means that the floor of the stock has now been raised from $9 to $11. This is important to note as you now expect the stock's price to hit $11 and then bounce back up. Here, you can use the "triple bottoms" indicator. This is exactly the same as the triple tops. You have three consecutive hits on the floor. This will determine the support level.

At this point, you can now confidently ride a rangebound trading strategy. Since you now have a reasonable belief regarding the range in which the stock will trade, you can place your next trades based on the new floor and ceiling.

This type of approach can be measured by using the 50-day and 200-day moving average. As such, you have enough data to determine how the trade will play out. Considering the length of the trade, you stand to make much more profit as compared to a day trading or swing trading approach.

Please keep in mind that all position trading strategies look to maximize profits based on historical data. If you base your trades on hunches, you may find that the price points you have anticipated may never materialize. Unless you have some reason to believe a stock that has never hit triple digits will do so at some point, then you are better off making your trades based on historical data. While the stock may reach the price point you expect, it may take years to get there. This is the reason why it is better to base your assumptions on real data. Otherwise, you may find yourself with an open position for far too long.

Only blue-chip stocks would be worth holding on to for any period greater than six months. Any other stock may become vulnerable to significant fluctuations. Naturally, this would pose unnecessary risk.

Chapter 11: Value Investing

Professional investors use value investing as a way to make under-the-radar moves. In value investing, investors search for value where others may not see it. Consequently, value investing is all about finding hidden gems.

This investment approach is quite popular among some of the most famous investors in the world. Warren Buffet, Benjamin Graham (Buffet's mentor), Charlie Munger, and David Dodd, among others, have built their investment strategy around value investing.

In essence, value investing consists of finding companies whose market value is below their intrinsic or book value. As such, these are companies that may have fallen on hard times but are poised to rebound at some point. Therefore, you must make an effort to go through financials and price history to determine a company's potential.

Determining Intrinsic Value

A company's intrinsic value is the value of its share capital based on its accounting. This means that a company is really worth what its accounting indicates. What you pay for in the open market is what investors believe it is worth. As such, there is always a difference between both numbers.

To determine a company's intrinsic value, all you need to do is take a company's total share capital and divide it by the number of outstanding shares. For instance, a company's total share value is $1,000,000. There are 100,000 outstanding shares. Therefore, 1,000,000 / 100,000 = 10. This means that each share is worth $10,

A company's intrinsic value changes very little over time. As a matter of fact, it's hard for companies to modify their intrinsic value as there are laws and accounting practices in place that limit this. Therefore, companies must be careful to follow proper accounting principles to ensure they are compliant with laws.

Determining Market Value

At the outset of this book, we explained how a company's market valuation depends on what investors believe the share price is worth. This is the reason why it changes so much in such a short time frame. Therefore, investors determine market value as a result of technical analysis. Of course, there are psychological factors involved. These factors determine whether a stock's valuation rises or falls.

Generally speaking, successful companies have a higher market valuation than intrinsic valuation. This implies that investors are prepared to pay more than the company is truly worth. The reasoning here is based on the company's potential for growth and profit.

When investors feel that a company is not performing up to expectations, its market valuation drops. In such cases, it's valuation may fall below its intrinsic value. In such cases, it could spell the end for the company. In many cases, companies don't rebound. Moreover, they may enter into bankruptcy proceedings. In some cases, companies emerge from restructuring. In others, the company is liquidated.

Spotting Potential Value

Spotting viable candidates for value investing takes time and research. Mainly, you need to pour over the company's financials. When you look at financials, you can get a glimpse into a company's overall health. If the company is generally profitable, but it is going through a tough time, then you can assume the company has a good chance of rebounding. By the same token, if you see bad financials, then the company may be headed for the glue factory.

Also, you must take a look at its price history. To get a good idea of where a company's valuation lies, look at its 200-day moving average. This will provide you with a very clear depiction of the company's true valuation. If you find that it has been in a bearish trend over the 200-day period, then you might be better off looking for another company. However, if you spot a clear moment where the stock took a downward turn, then you might have something.

Setting Up Your Trade

Please note that with value investing, there is no telling how long it will take a company to rebound. While it might take a few weeks, it might take a few months. It all depends on how quickly the company can rebound.

That being said, your entry point should be at the point where you see an MACD cross over. At this point, you will find the trendline crossing over the MACD line. When this happens, you might be on the verge of a trend reversal. Here, you must be ready to jump in and buy.

Next, it's time to determine your exit point. Technically, you could exit at any point above your entry point to make a profit. However, you are looking to maximize your profit. So, a good yardstick for your exit point would be to use the Fibonacci sequence. Look for the 61.8% level. This would be a very good exit point. Realistically, the 100% level may be unattainable, at least in the short term. As such, the 61.8% level would make perfect sense as it's slightly above the halfway mark of the stock's previous high. More conservative investors opt for the 50% level as an exit point.

Now, you can also use Fibonacci retracements to make multiple trades along the way. If the stock successfully rebounds, you can expect multiple pullbacks. Thus, using Fibonacci retracements can help you spot shorter-term trades.

On the whole, it is recommended that you make more conservative assessments. This is not the time to gamble. While it isn't easy to spot companies that might make a rebound, they can be quite profitable deals when you do spot them.

There is one caveat though. Please stay away from the so-called "penny stocks." Penny stocks are companies whose market valuation is less than $5. These are companies that are in liquidation. In the best of cases, they are zombie companies. This term means that they are still moving but not really going anywhere. As such, penny stocks are not worth your time as they will make very little profit if any. You could potentially make very short-term profits with penny stocks. However, it's best to look for companies which a much better chance of rebounding.

Conclusion

Thank you very much for making it all the way to the end of the book. If you're here, then it means you are serious about putting your money to work for you. By investing in the stock market, you are taking a huge step toward achieving your financial goals. As such, you are serious about making money without having to work any harder than you should.

So, what's the next step?

Please go over any sections of this book that you feel you need to review. Please keep in mind that reviewing specific parts of this book will help you improve your knowledge and experience. As you gain more and more experience, you'll be able to make the most of the information you have learned in this book.

It is also important to consider the options you have available to you. Often, it is not easy to make decisions given the vast array of options out there. This is the reason why it's important to ensure that you have all the information you need before making investment decisions. Moreover, please make sure that is careful with the so-called "gurus" and "experts." Thus, it is vital that you always verify the claims these individuals make. With this book, you can safely determine if the claims you hear are true or not.

The time has come for you to get started on the most exciting journey of your life. Stock market investing is the best way you can achieve your financial hopes and dreams. So, do take the time to carefully make your investment plan. As you set up your goals and aims, you will find that being realistic is the best place to start. As you gain more experience, you can set more ambitious goals. In the end, the sky is the limit when it comes to investing in the stock market.

Thank you once again for your time and dedication in reading this book. If you have found the information herein useful and informative, please tell your friends, colleagues, and family about it. They too will find this book to be useful. They will appreciate your sharing this information.

One last thing...

Stock market investing requires investors to do their homework. Please take the time to become familiar with technical analysis and fundamental analysis. The information you get from doing careful research will help you make the best possible investment decision. The good thing is that most of this research is done for you. Therefore, getting access to this information (usually through a subscription service) will help you make the most of the investment decisions you make. Often, spending a few extra dollars a month will make the difference between winning and losing trades.

Now that you're all set to go, please don't forget to have fun. In the end, if you enjoy investing, you will fare much better. By enjoying the time you spend investing, you will make much more money than you could have ever imagined!

OPTIONS TRADING FOR BEGINNERS

Introduction

Congratulations on purchasing *Options Trading for Beginners*, and thank you for doing so.

The concept of trading is often regarded as a very complex subject most of the time. But it is nothing like that. All you need is some calculation along with a bit of your intelligence. In this guidebook, you will find all the important aspects of options trading and how to start with the same. There are people who think of options trading as being risky and exotic. Also, those who have a huge bank balance can only invest in options. Well, this notion is completely wrong. You might think, how is this wrong? All your questions related to this 'HOW' will be answered in this guidebook. It does not matter what kind of an investor you are; options trading can turn out to be a superb source of income for anyone. It can provide you with excellent profits while also leveling up the structure of your portfolio.

It does not matter if your starting investment is very low. You can gradually improve the same with the help of options. Whenever there is a market downturn, it can also act as a shield of insurance for you. You will come across some superb strategies along with the basics of options trading that you can use in your portfolio. As soon as you end this book, you will feel like the king of options trading.

Chapter 1: History Of Options Trading

Many of you might think of options trading as a brand new form of investment in comparison to other forms of traditional investment like buying stocks and shares. The current form of options contract, as we all know today, was first introduced at the time when the Chicago Board Of Option Exchange or CBOE was established. However, the basic form of options trading is believed to be formed and established in ancient Greece, somewhat around the fourth century BC. From that ancient time, options have been reigning in the trading market in several forms until the CBOE was formed in 1973. From that year, options were standardized in a proper way for the first time. That was the time when options trading started gaining market credibility. Let us start with the history of options before we jump to the basics of options trading.

Olive Harvest And Thales

The earliest example related to options that were first recorded was referred to in a historical book written by a Greek Philosopher, Aristotle, in the mid 4th century BC. There are several books written by Aristotle on various subjects, and all his writings are of great historical influence. In his famous book 'Politics,' Aristotle decribed his account with another historical philosopher known as the Thales of Miletus. In that book, it was described how Thales profited from a huge olive harvest. He was an expert in astrology and mathematics. So, he tried to combine all his knowledge that he had on all the subjects to create the very first contract of options. By studying the position of the stars, Thales was able to predict that a huge olive harvest was going to take place in his region. So, he was all set for making some good profits from the predictions he made. He succeeded in recognizing that the demand for olive presses was going to rise. His motive was to corner the entire market.

However, despite all his calculations, Thales was facing difficulty in gathering sufficient funds for owning the olive presses in his area. So, he made a plan of paying all the owners of olive presses a certain amount of money to secure all his rights to use the presses at the correct time of harvesting. When the harvesting time arrived, as he already predicted earlier, the harvest of olives was huge. He then resold his rights that be bought from the owners of olive presses to all those people who were in great need of them. In this way, he was able to make some huge profits from his investment. Indeed, no form of the term was put into use at that time. Thales was the first one who created the first call option, where he used olive presses as the underlying asset.

Thales paid out all his right; however, it was not for the obligation to use the olive presses at a fixed rate. He was also able to exercise all the options that he had in possession to make a huge profit. All this is the basic principle of calls today. The only difference is that we have various other factors present in the game today. For example, financial instruments and commodities in the place of olive presses to act as an underlying asset.

Tulip Bulb Mania Of The 17th Century

Another great occurrence that can be linked to the history of options trading was a huge event in the 17th century. The event is known as the Tulip Bulb Mania that took place in Holland. At that time, tulips were quite popular in that area. In fact, it was regarded as a status symbol among the Dutch aristocrats. The popularity of tulips spread to the other parts of the world as well, along with Europe. All this craze for tulips resulted in a vast demand for tulip bulbs that gradually increased with passing time. However, by this time, calls and puts already got implemented in several markets, mainly because of hedging.

For example, the growers of tulips would purchase puts to safeguard the profits they make if there is a downfall in the rates of tulip bulbs suddenly. The tulip wholesalers opted for buying calls to safeguard themselves from the huge risk of rising rates of tulip bulbs. But all the contracts that were being used at that time were not that developed like today. Also, the market of options was not formal. In the 1630s, the overall demand of tulip bulbs skyrocketed. That lead to an increase in the price of bulbs than the actual value. The contracts of options for the price of bulbs also went up. As a result, a new market developed for dealing with all such contracts that permitted any person to speculate on the overall market of tulip bulbs. Most of the families in Holland opted for heavy investments in all such contracts. They either used up all their savings or by mortgaging their assets, such as property.

The price of tulip bulbs went up. However, it could only keep increasing until the time the tulip bulbs opened. The overall price of the tulip market increased to the point that it was of unsustainable nature. The tulip buyers disappeared from the market as the prices crashed heavily. Ordinary people lost everything they invested. The Dutch economy went into state of recession. As the options market was completely unregulated, there was no possible way for investors to fulfill the options contract obligations. All this created a bad name of options all over the world.

Brokers And Russell Sage

Some noteworthy development was brought forward in the history of options by Russell Sage, an American financer. During the later phase of the 19th century, he started developing calls and puts that could be easily traded in the U.S. over the counter. But no formal nature of the market was still available. However, Sage still opted for the development of an activity that is often regarded as a great breakthrough in the options trading market. Russell Sage was the first individual who developed a pricing relationship between the price of options, the price of underlying assets, and the interest rates. During the latter half of the 18th century, brokers and dealers started placing advertisements to get the attention of buyers and sellers of contracts with the aim of deal brokering. The primary idea was to create a link between the interested customers and a definite broker to either buy calls or puts on any specific stock.

The options market was continuously being regulated by the brokers only with the trading of contracts over the counter. The market was still illiquid, with only limited activity at this point. Some regulations were brought into the picture by the Securities And Exchange Commission. However, the scale of trading was not progressing, which was noticeable by the late 1960s. In 1968, a significant downfall was noticed in the Chicago trade board in the trading of commodities. Thus, the organization started searching for some brand new ways to develop the business. In the year 1973, the CBOE took up the venture of trading. The options contracts were standardized in the proper way for the very first time. Also, a fair marketplace was developed for trading options. The Options Clearing Corporation was also established at that time to take care of centralized clearing. It also made sure that the options contracts were fulfilled properly. After all this, options trading was taken to be legitimate.

Chapter 2: Basics Of Options

Before you start with trading, there are several important things that you will have to be aware of. In this chapter, you will find everything related to the basics of options trading. Indeed, there is a wide range of options that are available for investing, and also it comes with various types of financial instruments to accomplish all your goals of making profits. One of the primary tools related to finance is options. Options are very versatile in nature, along with being dynamic than stocks. You might have the question in your mind that how are options more dynamic than stocks? Well, the answer is that in the sector of stocks, you will get only two proper ways of making profits or money.

One is the long one, and the other is the short one. Following the long way, you will have to buy a stock and also wait for a very long time for the value of the stocks to go up. If you want to make some profit, you sell the same. In the short way, you will have to sell some of the shares of a company and then purchase the same shares at a lower price at a later stage. If you opt for options, there are several ways in which you can make some potential profits. You will get the chance to trade options not only on stocks but also on currencies, commodities, and various other indices. The majority of new traders opt for the market of stocks without gaining any kind of experience and education prior to investment. So, you will have to get some proper knowledge to make some good profits from the majority of your investments.

What Are Options?

Options are like any other instruments of finance. The majority of people refer to options as contracts. It is because when someone buys options, they actually gain all the right for trading the underlying assets related to that option within a particular date and also at a specific price. However, there is no fixed obligation for you to do so. In short, options are a mere form of security, just like a bond or stock. When it comes to the arena of options trading, you will come across two definite types of options contracts:

- **Call options:** You will get the chance of purchasing all the related underlying assets within a fixed time frame and at a specific rate.

- **Put options:** You will get the chance to sell all the related underlying assets within a fixed time frame and at a specific rate.

No matter which kind of option you opt for, both the contracts come with a predetermined selling or buying rate. The selling or buying price is known as the strike price. The date of expiry is the date when the overall validity of options comes to an end. After the expiry date, the option contract will turn out to be valueless. Before the contract reaches the expiry date, you will have all the right to hand over the same to someone else to make a nice profit. However, you will have to keep in mind that as there is time decay, the contract will be gradually losing its true value as it nears the expiry date. Every third Friday of any month is very important for any trader as in the majority of cases, Saturday is regarded as the expiry date that comes right next to the third Friday. The expiry date for the contract of options might vary. For example, the expiry date might turn out to be as long as a year for some options, whereas some of the options might have their expiry date at a very short term, like one week. In general, the traded options last for about one month to three months.

The component that is used for determining the price of the options contract is known as premium. The condition of the market will keep affecting the value of the premium constantly. It also depends on the overall performance of the underlying security. The time value, when added up with the intrinsic value, will provide you with the premium value. The time value will depend on the total time that is left before the expiry date. As already mentioned before, the more time left, the greater will be the time value. If you want to sell out an option, you will have to deduct the profit from the premium.

Options And Its Advantages

In the world of options trading, there are several advantages. Let's have a look at them.

- **Lesser financial commitment:** As you purchase some shares, you will have to give in a large amount of money. However, when it comes to options trading, the overall amount required for buying an option is comparatively less in comparison to the trading of stocks.

- **Lesser buyer pitfalls:** No matter if you want to buy a call option or a put option, you will have to continuously keep up with the trade. In case you make some incorrect decisions while figuring out the overall time frame, you will only lose the money that you have already paid to get the contract along with the trading fees.

- **More flexibility:** There are several strategies open right in front of the investors that they can effectively apply before the expiry date. They will get the chance to enhance their portfolio after exercising the contract and then purchasing the shares. They will also get the chance to sell either some or an entire portion of the shares that they bought or possess.

- **Determining the price of stock:** While discussing options trading, you, as the investor, will get the power to fix the price of the stock. In short, right before the expiry date, you will get the chance to sell or buy the stock at the determined strike price during any time that has been set.

Options And Its Disadvantages

Just like anything else in this world, options trading also includes some disadvantages.

- **Risk of great loss for all the sellers:** In the last section, we discussed that the buyer would not make any loss, regardless of what happens. However, when it comes to the aspect of the seller, they might face some huge losses. It is primarily because of the fact that when an investor writes calls or puts, they automatically come under the terms of trading the shares. It does not even depend on the market condition before the expiry date.

- **Decay of time:** Another great disadvantage of options trading is time decay. The closer an option gets to the date of expiry, the more will be the value of the loss. When the option reaches the expiry date, it will have zero value unless the option is being exercised in-the-money.

- **Constrained time:** In general, options are bound to play for the short term. So, all the investors will look out for movements in the short-term price to use the same in their favor. All these movements are required to take place within a fixed period of a few weeks to a few months. In fact, it might take place within a few days sometimes.

Styles Of Options

We have already discussed the basic types of options in the earlier sections. There are other option styles as well that we will learn about in this section. Most of the options that you will purchase will fall under any of these categories: American Options or European Options. Both of these are often referred to as vanilla options.

American Options

In this, you will get the chance to exercise the options any time before the expiry date. The majority of options on stocks and equity fall under this. All such contracts are the ones that can be traded for future exchanges.

European Options

Such options can be exercised on the expiry date only that has already been defined in the options contract. Such options are most often traded in the over-the-counter market.

Exotic Options

There are some option styles that are somewhat exotic than others.

Bermuda Options

Such options lie between American and European options. The options can be exercised on more than one date during the contract period.

Barrier Options

Such options are of completely different nature than the other types of options. In this, to pay off the price of the underlying security, it has to cross a particular level. They can be either a pull or a call option. Options of this nature are of four types:

- **Down-and-out:** It offers the holder every right but without any obligation to sell or purchase the shares of the underlying assets at a fixed strike price that has been predetermined until the price of the asset does not go below a certain barrier during the lifespan of the option. Once the asset price gets below the barrier, there will be no value of the option.

- **Down-and-in:** It is the complete opposite of the down-and-out option. It will carry a value only if the price of the underlying asset goes below a certain barrier during the lifespan of any option.

- **Up-and-out:** It is quite similar to the down-and-out option. The only difference between these two is the placement of the barrier. The options will be knocked out when the price of the underlying asset goes above the determined barrier.

- **Up-and-in:** It is quite similar to the down-and-in option. In this, the barrier placement is made above the underlying asset's current price. The option will be regarded as valid only when the underlying asset's price touches the determined barrier before expiration.

Chapter 3: Choosing Brokers

Options trading, at times, might take the shape of a complicated game. However, when you opt for a broker for your options with proper knowledge and care, you can be the master of the game quite easily. You will gain knowledge about conducting several types of research, tracking the positions, and placing trades. But there are some other essential things that you will have to take care of to find the perfect broker according to your needs.

Opting For Free Education

In case you are a beginner in the world of options trading or if you are willing to enhance all your trading strategies, looking out for a broker who can provide you with education regarding the same is essential. Education of this type can come in several forms:

- Online courses related to options trading
- Live or recorded webinars
- Face to face training
- Over the phone or online guidance

It is quite an effective idea to always be in the student-driver mode. Try to take in as much education as you can. If any broker provides you with a simulated version of their trading platform, you can also take a test drive of the entire process with the help of paper trading account. All this will help you to get a hold of everything before you start giving in your real money online.

Testing The Broker's Customer Service

Great and reliable customer service is essential if you are new to the trading world. A broker can be regarded as perfect when proper customer service is being provided. It is necessary for all those who are trying to opt for a new broker or are trying to get into the world of complex trades for which they need the help. First, you will have to start with the type of contact that you would like. Online live chat or email? Over the phone support? Is there any 24*7 service available for all sorts of technical glitches? Is the service available only on weekends? What kind of representative would you like to contact to answer all your queries related to your account?

The best thing that can be done on your part is to reach out to customer service and ask questions of your concern before you opt for applying for an account. All this will provide you with the necessary help to properly assess the caliber of the service. You can check whether the provided answers are satisfactory or if the response time is decent or not. The overall quality of a broker can be very easily assessed by the kind of customer service provided by them. Also, to be double sure, you can check out reviews of customer service online.

Ensuring That The Trading Platform Is Simple To Use

The platforms for options trading can be found in all types of shapes and sizes. The trading platforms can be desktop or online, web-based or software-based, have multiple platforms for providing basic and advanced training, offer full/ partial mobile functionality, or also a mixture of everything. You can start checking by visiting the broker website first. Try to find any guided tour of the platform or of the tools. Screenshots and video tutorials can also offer some functionality. However, trying out any simulated trading platform of the broker, if any is being offered, can help you gain the best knowledge regarding whether the broker is suitable for your use or not. Also, there are some other important things that you will have to consider.

- Is the overall design of the trading platform user-friendly? Are you required to hunt for the tools and things that you will need to trade?

- How easy is it to place any trade on the broker's platform?

- Is the trading platform capable and suitable for meeting all your needs? For example, setting alerts relying on any specific criteria or allowing you fill up a trade ticket in much advance to submit at a later time.

- Will you need mobile access for the full-service suite as you travel? Will a pared-down version of the trading platform be enough for you?

- How fast are the orders executed on the website? Is the broker's website reliable? All of this needs to be at the top of the priority list if your game is to enter and exit the positions quickly.

- Do you need to pay any monthly or annual fee for the trading platform? If yes, is there any possible way of waiving that fee? For example, by maintaining a minimum balance in your account or by opting for a certain number of trades within a specified period?

Proper Assessment Of Breadth, Costs, And Depth Of Data And Tools

Data and research are two things that are always regarded as the lifeblood of an options trader. There are some basic things that you will have to take care of.

- A feed of quotes that is frequently updated

- Basic type of charting to help you select the points of entry and exit

- Screening tools

- The ability to properly analyze the reward nature along with trade risks

If you are trying to opt for an advanced nature of trading, your strategies will need deeper trade modeling, along with analytical tools. All such tools include real-time market data from several providers, customizable types of screeners, and the capability of testing, developing, tracking, and back-testing trading strategies. Try to ensure whether the fancy tools are going to cost you extra. For instance, there are several brokers who can provide you with delayed quotes without any extra cost, lagging behind the market data by twenty minutes, but charges extra for real-time updated feed. Similarly, there are certain tools that are of expert level and are available to those customers only who can meet certain monthly or quarterly trading activity.

Not Weighing The Price Of Commission Heavily

As commissions can give you the chance to compare other brokers side-by-side, they are the primary things that most traders search for before picking a proper broker. You will have to regard certain things related to commissions charged by a broker.

- There are two primary components that determine the commission of options trading. They are base rate and per-contract fee. It is similar to the trading commission that an investor has to pay at the time of purchasing a stock.

- Some brokers also couple the per-contract fee and the trading commission within one single flat fee.

- There are brokers who provide discounted commissions depending on several things like frequency of trading, trading volume, and average maintained balance in the account.

In case you are a beginner or completely new to the trading world, or you just use the strategies rarely, a broker who offers one flat trading rate or the one that comes with no form of commission will be the best choice for you.

Trading Platforms

If you want to earn some good profits, opting for the perfect trading platform is very important. Here are some trading platforms that you can use effectively for a seamless trading experience.

Tastyworks

If you are a frequent trader, this platform can turn out to be your best companion. It comes with several tools that will offer you probability, liquidity, and volatility. Opening up a trading account on this platform is seamless. After you have created your account successfully, you will have to download the trading platform. Before trading, you can try out the different tools for getting a hold of the same. The cost per leg on this platform is $0. The cost will be $1 for each leg for opening a position, where the maximum can be $10 for each leg. Closing the position will cost $0.

Ally Invest

The best aspect of this platform is its low-cost brokerage. Also, there is no need to maintain a minimum account balance. Ally Invest supports the functioning of this platform. You can place orders on this platform within seconds. You can also modify all your settings, opt for technical analysis, and view necessary charts.

E*Trade

E* Trade's platform is the most advanced of all that can provide you with all your required tools. The per-contract commission here is $0.65. If you place more than 30 trades in a single quarter, the commission will be $0.50 for each contract. If the price of the contract is equal to or less than $0.10, any kind of fee is waived off.

Chapter 4: Management Of Risk

A very important thing in the game of options trading is properly managing the capital and exposure to risk. Indeed, risk can be easily avoided in all forms of investment, so risk exposure is not regarded as such a problem. The key here is to manage the risk funds effectively and ensure that you are totally comfortable with the level of risk you will take. You will also need to ensure that you are not exposing the capital and yourself to any form of unsustainable losses. All of this also applies to the management of money. You are needed to start trading by only using that amount of capital that you can afford to lose without overstretching your capabilities. As effective management of risk and money is crucial for successful options trading, you will have to understand the subject properly. You will be gaining all forms of knowledge and some methods in this chapter that will help you manage risk exposure and control the trading budget.

Opting For A Trade Plan

One of the important aspects in the world of trading is to have in possession a proper trading plan that comes with all the required guidelines and parameters for all sorts of trading activities. The main usage of having a trading plan is to provide you with the necessary help to manage risk exposure and your money. The plan of trading that you are going to design for yourself needs to have every possible detail about the trade – starting from the risk level that you are capable of taking to the total amount that you can put into use. As you start trading by following the plan and set up your mind to use that amount of money that you can truly invest in setting up trading of options, you will be able to stay safe from the greatest mistake. The mistake is to put into use cared money.

When you enter the ring of trading with that amount of money that you cannot afford to lose, or you have kept it aside for fulfilling something else, you will have lesser chances of going for any kind of rational decision in your trades. It is true that it is hard to remove any kind of emotions involved in options trading. You will have to be focused as much as you can on those things that you tend to do, along with the reason behind doing the same. As you permit emotions to take over all the control, the chances are high that you will easily lose all the concentration. You might also start behaving irrationally. It can make you chase all your losses from the past trades that went bad or just make all those transactions that you would not have opted for usually. If you keep following the set plan and use the determined capital, you will get the chance to keep all your irrational emotions under your control.

You will also have to adhere to the level of risk that you have already included in your plan. If you want to opt for trades that come with lower risk only, there is no proper reason to try to expose yourself to all those trades that come with higher risk. You might find it quite tempting at times, only because you have experienced a very small amount of loss till now. It might also happen if you try to fix all your losses or when you have done great with any of your low-risk trades. Now, all you are willing to do is enhance the profit level as quickly as possible. But if you have already planned to make or get involved in trades of low risk only, there has to be some reason for doing so. There is nothing good in pushing yourself out from the comfort zone only because of your emotional reasons, as already discussed before.

There are useful ways in which you can manage risks in options trading.

Management Of Risk Using Options Spreads

One of the most effective and strong tools that can be found in options trading is options spreads. It is nothing but when you begin combining more than a single position on the options contracts, which is based on the same underlying asset to create an overall trading position. For example, if you purchase money calls on some specific stock and then opt for writing cheaper out-of-the-money calls once again on a similar stock, you will be creating an option spread called bull call spread. Purchasing in calls indicates that you will get the chance to profit something if the underlying stock value goes up. However, you will lose something or all the money that you have already spent in purchasing them if the underlying stock value does not rise. As you write calls on the same stock, you will get control of some of the starting costs. In this way, you will get the chance to reduce the money that you might lose.

Every strategy of options trading includes using spreads. Spreads can provide you with a great way to manage the risks. You can start using them to reduce the upfront costs of entering positions. You will also be able to reduce the money that you might lose, just like the example of a bull call spread as discussed above. In short, you can get the power to reduce all forms of profits that you might make, along with reducing the overall risk percentage. Spreads can be used to reduce all forms of risks that can be found while entering any short position. For example, if you decide to write puts on a specific stock, you will be able to get a payment upfront just for writing the options. However, you will also increase your exposure to all forms of potential losses in case the stock tends to decline the value. If you opt for purchasing cheaper out of money puts, you will have to put into use a part of the upfront payment.

You can get the chance of preventing any kind of potential loss that might be caused by any decline in the stock. The spread of this type is called a bull put spread. After you have checked both the examples, you can find that it is possible to get into positions where you have got the chance to still gain some amount of profit if the stock price moves in the correct direction. However, you will be able to limit all your losses if the stock price starts going against you. It is the primary reason why traders try to use spreads so often for trading options. They can act as great devices to manage risks effectively.

Management Of Risk Using Diversification

Diversification is another effective technique of managing risks that is widely used today by all investors who are trying to build up their portfolio of stocks by using the idea of hold and buy. The basic functioning of the technique of diversification is to properly spread all the investments over several companies and sectors to create a balanced nature of portfolio. The concept of putting an excessive amount of money into one particular company or sector is avoided. When you have a portfolio of diversified nature, you will have fewer chances to get exposed to any kind of risk than a portfolio built up with only one type of investment. When it comes to the game of options trading, diversification is not considered to be that important. However, it has still got some uses that can help in diversification in several ways.

The principle of functioning remains the same more or less; you would not want to direct an excessive amount of capital for one particular investment only. You can use diversification in options trading in various methods. You can begin diversifying by using a wide collection of strategies, trading a number of options that rely on several types of underlying assets, and opting for trading several types of options. In short, the primary idea of diversification is to let you make profits in several ways. You will not need to rely completely only on one particular outcome for all your trades to be a success.

Management Of Risk Using Options Orders

A simple way of risk management is to utilize several ranges of various order types that you can place. Along with the four primary order types that can be used for opening and closing positions, there are some other types of orders that you can place. Most of such orders can help you to properly manage the risks involved. For instance, a general type of market order will get filled up at the best price right at the time of execution. It is the most generic way of selling and purchasing options. However, in a market that is volatile in nature, all the orders might tend to get filled up at a price point that is either higher or lower than you want them to be. By utilizing limit orders, where you can get the power of setting up the minimum and maximum prices at which your concerned order can be filled, you can avoid purchasing or selling at prices that are not of favorable nature.

Also, there are orders that you can use to automate the task of exiting a position. It does not matter whether that is to lower the losses on any specific trade that failed to function properly for you or to lock in the probable profits you have already made. By utilizing orders like a market stop order, trailing stop order, or limit stop order, you will get the power to effectively control your point of exit at any position. You will also be able to limit the risk percentage to which you are exposed to on the trades that you want to make.

Money Management And Position Sizing

Money management is directly linked to risk management. Both of these two are essential on the same scale. You will have a certain amount of money that you can use. So, it is of great importance to have proper control on the capital budget. You will have to make sure that you do not just end up losing all you have and then placing yourself in a suffocating position where you can no longer get involved in trading. The perfect way of money management that you already have in your hand is by opting for the simple concept of position sizing. It involves the process of determining the part of the capital that you have in hand to be used in entering a particular position.

To make position sizing the most effective, you will have to take care of the amount of money you truly want to invest in any possible form of trade concerning the percentage of the entire capital investment. Many people also regard the position to be somewhat similar to that of diversification in several aspects. By deciding to use up a small percentage of the in-hand capital in one form of trade, it will be foolish of you to depend only on one specific outcome. Even all the professional traders who are quite successful in the market will make the mistake of making trades that might result badly with time. The key over here is to ensure that the bad trades cannot affect you much worse.

For instance, if you make up your mind to use 50% of the total in-hand capital in one trade only, and it results in a complete loss, you will lose a great amount of funds that you have. In place of doing that, try to use 12% - 15% of your capital for each trade. Even if you make recurring losses, the losses will not be able to destroy you.

Chapter 5: Covered Calls

The covered call is quite a common strategy that can be used in options trading. It can be used when you have some stocks in your possession. You can sell at-the-money or out-of-the-money calls in the same proportion to the shares in hand. For example, you have 1000 shares of DEF stock. You will be able to sell a maximum of 10 calls in a covered call transaction. A buy-write, also known as call write, is a useful strategy that belongs to the covered call strategy. In this, the purchasing of stocks and selling out of options will be a part of the same transaction. The platform of trading that you are going to use might have the ability to execute a buy-write order. For instance, the selling price of any call is set at $2, and the stock is traded at a price of $100, you will be able to enter one single order to execute the entire transaction at a price of $98 or even more than that.

When you decide to enter a limit order in this manner, you will not be able to execute on one side of the entire transaction unless the other side is also executed. As you sell out a covered call, you will get the chance to profit from three basic sources:

- Premium of the option
- Increase in the price of the underlying asset
- Stock dividends

An option position is generally regarded as being covered, for this purpose, when an offsetting is available in the opposite position of the market, for example, long stock. You will have to note that one downside of a covered call is its incapability to earn interest on all those proceeds that are used up to purchase the stocks. However, you will be entitled to get the dividends if you own the stocks. A covered option comes with various risks. For instance, if a trader is long 100 shares of a certain stock that is also being traded at a rate of $100 for each share, and he decides to sell one call at $2 ($200). At that time, the stock price goes up to $50 for each share; the trader will lose $50,000 in total long stock. The trader will receive a premium that will function as a consolation gift only.

Basics Of Covered Call

A covered call can serve as the hedge of either short-term or any position of long stock. It lets the investors to get their income through the received premium after writing any option. But the investor will forfeit all the gains from the stocks if the price of the stock goes above the option's strike price. In case the buyer makes up his mind to exercise an option, the investors will have to provide a total of 100 shares at the option's strike price. The covered call strategy will not be useful for any investor who is bullish or bearish. If an investor is excessively bullish, they will tend not to sell out the price and try to hold back the overall stock.

The profit will be provided by the option on the entire stock, which might lower the entire profit from the trade if the price of the stock goes up. Just like that, when an investor is excessively bearish in nature, they might tend to sell off all their stocks. It is because the premium that the investor will receive for selling out a call will help to offset the entire loss on that particular stock if the price of the stock goes down.

How Can You Profit From Covered Calls?

The buyer will pay the call option seller a premium to get the complete right to purchase the shares or contracts at a price determined already. The premium is nothing but the cash fee, which is paid out on the day when an option is sold. It is also the amount of money that the seller will keep, no matter if the option is exercised or not.

When Is The Right Time To Sell Covered Calls?

As you decide to sell out a covered call, you will get the payment in exchange for leaving a position that might rise in the future. For example, you purchase stocks of DEF at $50 for each share with the belief that it might go up to $60 within a period of 365 days. You might also have the urge to sell out the same at a rate of $55 after a period of 6 months. All of this can easily bring in a short-term profit. In such a case, selling the covered calls on any position might turn out to be a superb strategy. The stock options chain will show that selling an option that is six months old for $55 will cost the buyer a premium of $4 for each share. You will have the choice to sell the option against all your shares, which you have bought for $50 previously, with the hope that you can sell the same, next year, at $60.

Writing this particular call option will result in the creation of an obligation to sell out all the shares at a price of $55 within a period of six months if the price of the underlying asset reaches the same level. You will get the opportunity to keep the premium of $4, along with $55 from the selling shares. So, the total amount will be $59 or a return of 18% within six months. On the other side, you will face a loss of $10 on the position if the stock price comes down to $40. But you will still have the chance to keep the premium of $4 that you will get after you sell out a call option. In this very way, you will be able to lower the overall loss from $10 to $6 for each share. Selling covered calls can help you in offsetting the downside risk or even add up to the upside return, taking along the premium in exchange for any rise in the future above the strike price of the option in addition to the premium.

Chapter 6: Putting Into Use The Collar Strategy

Collar, also known as the hedge wrapper, is a well-known options trading strategy that is most often implemented by investors to protect themselves from huge losses. However, you will also need to keep in mind that it can limit huge gains. As an effective investor, you will get the chance to create a collar position by simply getting an out-of-the-money put option and selling out an out-of-the-money call. The put will protect you if, in any case, the price of the stock tends to go down. As you sell out the call options, you will get the income, and it will also let you earn some profit on that stock, which is limited to the call option's strike price. You cannot earn more than that.

Collar Strategy In Detail

Any investor can decide to execute a collar whenever they have in possession a long-term stock that has not returned any kind of substantial gains or profits. Also, an investor might decide to use the strategy of the collar if they are sure regarding the stock in the long run; however, they are not sure of the prospects in the short-term. To protect the profits from any kind of downwards movement of the stock, the strategy of collar can be successfully implemented. The best-case scenario for an investor will be when the underlying asset's overall price is also the same as the strike price of the call option that has been sold out before the expiration date. The strategy of the collar is composed of two varying strategies: one is the protective put, and the other is the covered call. We have already discussed covered call in the last chapter. A protective put or married put includes staying with an option of put, along with the underlying securities. A covered call includes being short of a call option and also being long for the securities.

The purchasing of an out-of-the-money put option is everything that can help an investor with the necessary protection from any form of potential downfall in the stock price. Selling out a call option of out-of-the-money type will help in the generation of premiums that have already been paid while purchasing the put. Both call and put will have to be of the same expiry month, along with the same contract numbers. The put that has been bought will require having a strike price, which is much lower than the current stock's market price. The call that is being sold out will require a strike price much above the current stock's market price. In fact, the trade will have to be developed for little or zero out-of-the-pocket cost in case you decide to select the respective strike price that is at an equal distance from the present price of the owned stock. As they will be taking a risk by significantly sacrificing all their gains from the stocks above the covered call's strike price, the collar strategy is not a good choice for those investors who are excessively bullish on their stocks.

Break Even Point And Collar Profit Loss

The break even point or BEP of any investor on this strategy is the sum total of all the premium that he has received and also been paid for the call option or put option added or subtracted to/from the purchase price of all the underlying securities relying on whether there is debit/credit. The net credit can be determined when the premiums that have been received are more than the overall premiums that have been paid. The net debit can be determined when the total premiums paid are more than the received premium.

BEP = Underlying asset purchase price + Total debit

BEP = Underlying asset purchase price − Total credit

The overall profit from the collar is equal to the call's strike price minus the stock purchase price per share of the underlying asset. The options cost, whether debit or credit, will be the dividend. The maximum loss will be the purchasing rate of the underlying asset minus the strike price of the put. The option cost will be factored in after that.

Maximum profit = (Call strike price − Net put/Call premiums) − Stock purchase price

Maximum loss = Stock purchase price − (Put strike price − Net put/Call premiums)

Example Of Collar

Suppose you are a trader who is long of XYZ stock by 1000 shares at a fixed price of $80 for each share. The current trading price of the stock is $87 per share. You decide to temporarily hedge your position as there is an increase in the trading market's overall volatility. You purchase 10 puts (one option contract is equal to 100 shares) with the strike price of $77. You sell out 10 calls with the strike price of $97. Your cost for collar implementation (sell the call at $87 and purchase the put at $77) will be a debit of $1.50 for each share.

BEP = $80 + $1.50 = $81.50 each share

The maximum profit that you can earn over here is $15,500 or 10 options contracts x 100 shares x (($80 − ($97 - $1.50)). It will happen if the stock price goes to $97 or even more than that. The maximum loss that you might face is $4,500 or 10 x 100 x (($77 - $1.50) - $80). It will happen if the stock price goes to $77 or even less than that.

Forecasting Market

Perfect market forecast for collar strategy depends on the purchasing time of the stock, which is also relative to the option's entry positions. It also depends on the willingness of a trader to sell the stock. If any collar position is established by first acquiring the shares, there will be a need for a 2-part forecast. The forecast will have to be entirely neutral from bullish. There is a great need for a proper reason to limit the risks. On the contrary, when a collar is developed to protect any pre-existing holding on a stock, there will be two probable scenarios. The short-term forecast might turn out to be bearish, and the long-term forecast can be bullish. Secondly, the trader might get close to the target selling price of the concerned stock.

Chapter 7: Call Spreads

In call spread, you do not have to develop a stock position. In place of that, you will get the chance to play one strike price against the other. The only disadvantage of this is that you will require having a definite bias of the market. So, they are not completely market neutral from the perspective of a strategy. The inevitable truth is that none of the strategies that are available today is 100% market neutral. But, from the perspective of risk, they can easily insulate you from the sudden movements of the market. That is why it is essential to get to know about all such strategies in detail. Let us have a look at the functioning of call spreads.

Bull Call Spread

The bull call spread will assume that you possess a bullish view on the overall market based on technical analysis. The best part about this very strategy is that it can be very easily adjusted, similar to a collar. However, there is no requirement to establish a long stock position. Indeed, all strategies related to spread come along with the inherent advantage. The strategy of bull call spread can work the best in markets that have been titled as bullish, but in actuality, it is not so. What I am trying to say is that the market often heads in one direction; however, you will notice that it drifts about, diving much often as it rises above with a very small push upwards.

See-saw movement of this sort is a perfect thing for a bull call spread. It can even work in strong bull markets. But personally, I would suggest you to go long on a call for capturing the entire movement. You will have to remember that strong bullish movements of this type tend to happen very rarely. So, you will have to decide and choose with proper care. Let us dive deeper into the functioning of this strategy.

Execution

The bull call spread comes along with two legs:

- A long in or at-the-money call
- A short out-of-the-money call

The main generator of profit in this strategy is the long call. It is all that will capture the stocks' upward movement. It will allow you to earn an increased premium through the enhanced intrinsic value of the concerned option. The short call will be your profit goal effectively or might be a little beyond that. It will increase your total profit along with your earn income from the very premium after writing it. Let us see how the math actually works by taking the example of the AMZN. The market price is set at $1833.51. So, for establishing the first leg of the trade, you will have to choose an at the money or in the money option from the contracts of the near month. The closest that is possible to get is 1835, which is offered out at $63.65 for each share.

Now, what would be the correct target price? Well, it will depend on the way you will be reading the market. If it is going sideways, with a little bit of bullish title, placing the target right at the range boundary will be the best idea. Indeed, your short call will have to be much beyond this very limit. Let's assume our target is set at $1862. It will make writing the strike call at 1865 a great option. The premium that you can get for writing the option will be $44.55 for each share. How does the math work?

Trade entry cost = Long call cost − Short call premium = 63.65 − 44.55 = $19.10 each share

Maximum profit = Short call's strike price − Strike price of long call = 1865 − 1835 =$30 each share

Your trade entry will be the maximum possible loss as if the stock price goes down, as it might be the worst-case scenario, your long call will expire worthless. You will get the chance to keep the entire premium from the short call. Your maximum profit will be capped by the short call's strike price. There is nothing that you need to be worried about the moving of short calls into the money. It is primarily because you will have the lower long call covering this very position. In such a case, you will simply need to exercise the lower call and also use the same to fulfill the exercise of the higher call. The ratio of reward to risk for this particular example will be quite decent, if not amazing.

You will have to note that this very strategy takes full advantage of the non-committal or sluggish markets with a little bullish tilt towards them. In all such markets, a trader who is directional in nature will have a high chance of getting wiped out.

Adjustment

It is actually possible to adjust the bull call spread. Also, all of this will depend on your level of confidence regarding your analysis. The adjustment over here is quite similar to that of the collar. First, you will have to cover a short call position for earning a profit, as the premium might decrease. Secondly, you close out a long call for a loss as it is now going to be out of the money. After all the things are set equal, the long call loss will be offset by the profit that you will get from closing a short call. So, you are still in trade till now. You can reestablish a long call right from a new market level and can determine whether you want to maintain the same target price or just change it.

Bear Call Spread

Just like the bull call spread strategy takes full advantage of the sluggish bull markets, this strategy takes advantage of the sluggish bear markets. The perfect time to put both the strategies into action is right towards the end, where the participation of a counter trend is getting higher by every minute. The market will move into a distributive or accumulative phase to prepare for the trend change. All this happens to be the real market state for the majority of the part. So, you can be assured that both strategies can work great for you. The strategy of bear call spread can also work in a sideways market. In this, the best place to implement is near the topmost end of the sideways range. Let us dive deeper into the execution of this strategy.

Execution

The bear call spread comes with two proper legs:

- A near the money or at the money short call

- A long call of out of the money

The main instrument for earning profit is the short call, which will take advantage of the decreasing price as the long call caps the downside. The main factor of earning in this trade will be the premium that you can earn on writing a short call. Just like the bull call, the maximum loss and profit are capped. All this will provide you with a superb view of the trade probabilities right off your bat. Let us find out how this strategy will work with the present levels of AMZN. With the market price of $1833.50, the closest money call in the far month will be 1835 strike call. As you write this, it will provide you with a premium of $60.15 for each share. When it comes to the point of determining the long call's strike price, you would like to place this much beyond the closest resistance level. Suppose it happens to be at 1840 level. The overall premium for this be $58.10 for each share. How does the math work?

Trade entry cost = Long call's cost − Premium from short call = 58.1 − 60.15 = -$2.05 (you will earn this on the entry)

Maximum loss = Long call's strike price − Short call's strike price = 1840 − 1835 =$5 each share

Maximum gain = Trade entry cost

The maximum possible gain that you can have from this trade is the premium of the short call. But the long call will also decrease in price simultaneously. So, they will tend to offset each other. As it can be seen, the risk/reward profile is altered for this very strategy, with the risk being much greater in comparison to the reward.

Then, why should someone pursue this? First of all, you will require to understand that the rate of success for this strategy will depend on how well you are able to read the conditions of the market. If the condition of the market is bearish, it will be better for you to purchase a put in place of putting into use the bear call spread. It is the fact that you will be able to generate huge profits in sluggish markets that makes this so attractive in nature.

Adjustment

Is it possible to adjust this kind of trade? The answer is YES. Similar to the bull call spread, in case the market goes in the opposite direction, you can move the spread higher and have the initial legs offset each other either by exercising them or closing them. You can also take the greatest loss and just move on.

Calendar Call Spread

The spreads that we have discussed till now are known as vertical spreads. It implies the way they show up on the chain of options, where the strike prices are properly listed on top of each other. By buying one and shorting another, you will earn the difference between the two. That is why it is termed as 'spread.' Vertical trades will need you to trade the options within the same month of expiry. But in horizontal spreads, which is all about the calendar spread, includes selling and buying the options from various months of expiry. It is a bullish strategy that can be used largely in your favor.

Execution

The strategy of calendar call spread comes with two legs:

- A short term or current month call
- A long term or near month call

The main idea is that when the stock takes time to make itself to the call's longer strike price, you can collect a short call premium in the meantime. The longer call acts as the instrument of profit, which will capture the stock's upward movement.

The longer-term call can either be something from the longer cycle or the near month. The choice will be yours completely. The only thing that you will have to consider over here is the liquidity, as you would not want to trade in an instrument that comes with a huge spread. As long as the spreads are manageable or low, and the liquidity is fine, you will be fine. Let us find out how the math gets implemented with AMZN.

Suppose the long call is from the near month. The price that you will pay for the call of 1830, which is the nearest to the market price, is $63.65. For the short call, let's assume there is a medium resistance of 1840. The premium that you will earn on this very call is $36.30.

The entry cost = long call's cost − premium from the short call = 63.65 − 36.3 = $27.35 each share

Maximum loss = Entry cost

There are several scenarios to calculate the maximum profit, as you can actually imagine. It is because it relies on whether the call of the short term ever moves into the money. No matter what the scenario is, you are required to subtract the entry cost from the overall final gain. Thus, horizontal spreads are completely different from vertical spreads because of their open-ended nature.

Chapter 8: Put Spreads

Like the call spreads that permit you to make some good money in every market condition, put spreads will also let you do the same. Most of the traders and brokers prefer using put spreads as there is a lesser chance of any fat finger error, resulting in great risk exposure. For instance, with the strategy of call spreads, if you decide to enter the short call much before even covering the legs of long calls, you will be triggering all types of alarms at the broker headquarter. Is there are any kind of inherent advantage to put spreads over the calls? Well, it will depend largely on the trader type. There are traders who are always hesitant to opt for puts execution. It is because they think a put explicitly gains from a downside movement in the stock where any short call earns only the premium.

It is a very common sentiment among all those who are new to the trading world, and I would like to end such sentiments. There is nothing unethical or wrong in profiting from a downswing. If there is anything, it is only because of economics. If there was no existence of downswings, you would have totally unstable markets. Just like call spreads, put spreads also lend themselves to bearish, bullish, and sideways strategies very well.

Bear Put Spread

The bear put trade tries to take advantage of the bearish markets. In contrast to the bullish markets that come with varying degrees, bearish nature markets tend to have lesser degrees of strength. In simple terms, while a market of bullish nature can be classified according to several levels, ranging from extremely bullish to slightly bullish, bear markets would lend only to three or two such classifications.

The reason behind this is quite straightforward. The large majority of institutional activity and the general public are focused only on the long side of the concerned market. So, when such institutions try to conduct their campaigns of purchase, you can notice a greater degree of fluctuation within any specified stock as it rises up. The fact that several traders are always involved in producing more scenarios of price behavior and all these results in a larger number of trend level strength.

In contrast, bearish markets involve far lesser traders. You will never find a bear market opting to make up its mind when it leans towards going downward. Distribution movements, which generally occur before a trend of the bear, do not last long. Bear trends also run faster and exhaust themselves much sooner in comparison to bull trends. The main point over here is that you will have to be on your own with the bear markets. We have already discussed the bear call spread in the last chapter that takes full advantage of the sluggish points of the trend of a bear. The bear put also aims to do the same; however, there are some differences in the way they try to play out themselves.

Execution

The bear put comes with two legs:

- Long put near or at the money

- Short put below the long out of the money

The main instrument of gain over here is the long put, which will be appreciated when the price of the stock decreases. The aim of the short put is to reduce the cost of carrying long put through the earned premium upon writing it. Let us have a look at AMZN to figure out how it works.

The current trading price of AMZN is 1833.51. Let us assume that the trend of bear in this very stock is going to show some signs of getting slow. It is slowly approaching a strong level of support that is not likely to go past. You can learn the identification signs later. At this moment, try to commit to the memory and also note to refer to them at a later phase. The closest at the money put is the 1835 strike price the near month put, which also has an asking price of $53.80 for each share. It is the long portion of this trade. Now, you will have to determine which level will be the perfect one for short. We have seen that a strong level of support is close by that is most unlikely to get breached. Can you use this as the short level? Let us say that this is at $1800. The starting bid for this very put is $39.85 for each share. The math will work out in this way:

Entry cost = Long put cost − Premium from the short = 53.8 − 39.85 = $13.95 for each share

Maximum profit = Difference between the strike prices of long and short put = 1835 − 1800 = $35 for each share

The maximum amount of loss is equal to the entry cost as the premium changes of both the puts will effectively offset each other. As the price goes up, the long put will go down in price, while the short put will go down as well by a similar rate. Thus, you will get a profit that will offset the overall loss on the trade's long leg. By this point, you must have become familiar with successfully working out the spread trade math. Now, you can also see how the dynamics of the same will work. In regards to adjustment, it will work in the same way with the bear put as it tends to do with the bear call. In case the price goes up and takes the long put out of money, you will have to recheck whether your analysis was perfect or not.

In case you think that it holds, you can opt for closing the short, which can provide you with a profit for offsetting the long portion, which will be closed out as well. Try to establish a brand new spread or just maintain the short at the exact level. Keep a note that you can always close out long put and also go along at a higher rate without even touching the short if you desire to maintain it at the same level. The criterion that you will have to follow is exactly the same as the trades of call spreads. The decision that you will make will rely on the factors of technical analysis that you see and also how well you can deduce conclusions from all of them. You will face one more choice, now that you have gained knowledge of how a bear put functions, would you choose a bear put spread or a bear call spread. Both strategies take advantage of the same market conditions. So, which one would you opt for?

Bull Put Spread

Bull put spreads are quite useful in taking advantage of the sluggish uptrends or even sideways movements with a bit of upward tilt towards them.

Execution

Bull put spread comes with two legs:

- Short at the money or in the money put

- Long out of the money put some levels right below the short

The short put is that leg that tries to take advantage of the price rise. The long put can cover your downside if the market sentiment is in your opposition. As you successfully enter the trade, you will be able to earn the premium from put and have to pay for entering the long put. The only difference between the two is the entry cost along with the maximum profit. Your maximum loss is the direct difference between the strike prices of both the legs. In case the strike price falls and brings the long put into the money, your downside will get capped at that level. So, when you enter this trade, you will get a net credit or money. If you try to compare this with bear put, it is a net debit. In short, you will have to pay money to be in the trade. Let us have a look at an example of AMZN.

The price of the market is still the same. However, in this case, the environment is a bit different. The environment is bullish in nature, which is moving upwards sluggishly. The closest at the money put to short is the level 1835. It will provide you with $53.30 for each share. Let us assume that the level of support is 1800. So, the cost needed to go long will be $40.40.

Entry cost = Long put cost − Premium earned from short put = 40.4 − 53.3 = -12.90 for each share

Maximum loss = Short put's strike price − Long put's strike price = $35 each share

Similar to the bear call, the ratio of reward to risk is altered. If you want to make some kind of adjustments to the trade, the criteria are exactly the same as before.

Chapter 9: Common Mistakes Of Beginners

Options are considered a great tool for trading that provides you with the flexibility to use the same in any market condition. You can use options either for generating income, producing good profits, or hedging risks. However, there are some common mistakes in options trading that are mostly made by beginners as they step into the trading world. If not used in the correct way, options can easily erode all that you have in your account. Even it can create margin calls, which is regarded as the worst-case scenario. So, let us have a look at some of the most common mistakes made by beginners that you will have to avoid for your own good.

Focusing On OTM Options

Out-of-the-money or OTM call or put options are much cheaper in comparison to others. So, the majority of new traders think of them as a great deal. Indeed, it is true in some cases, options are priced all the time in such a way that you can never get a tasty dinner for free. The premium or value of the option as you purchase it will keep decaying with passing time. So, not only the price of the option is required to go above or below the strike price, the same needs to be done before the expiration date as well. In actuality, it might result in being a daunting task for making consistent money with the help of this approach. There are times when OTM options trading is only a form of strategy.

It will be really foolish of you if you get stuck in the trap while thinking that as the price of the option is low, it will be a better deal than others. You will have to assess all kinds of probability to check that the underlying asset's price will not go above the strike price before the date of expiry, depending on past tendencies before you buy OTM options.

No Proper Exit Plan

One of the major mistakes made by beginner traders is that they do not possess a proper exit plan. As you opt for a particular trade, you are expecting to earn some money. But how much? How will you determine that the amount of profit is perfect? If an option is on the verge of expiring worthlessly, is it a better option to sell it off much before? Will it be able to reduce the overall loss? Will you stick to the option until the expiration date? All of these, along with many other questions, are required to be addressed before making a trade. Doing these at the time of making the trade is not at all a healthy decision. You will have to be sure of your profit target by tracking the past security movements. You will have to determine some ways in which you can reduce the overall risk. Also, being sure of when to exit the trade is very important.

Not Being Attentive To Small Gains For The Huge Gains

All of us love to enjoy the feeling of making huge gains in a trade. It is very simple and easy to look at the home run trades. But it is actually harder to earn so. The majority of the time, stocks do nothing, and it is quite tough to determine when any of such stocks are going to make a big explosion. Markets keep changing the percentage points continuously. So, you can say that it is quite easier to earn small returns consistently rather than waiting for the big return. Indeed, making 2% only every week by following a fixed strategy is not at all attractive, like making 20% each week. However, piling up various 2% per week is much better than waiting for a huge return.

You need to note that you are building up your capital slowly when you keep making small gains continuously. It will help largely in producing compound returns. On the other hand, when you lose some big trade, you will keep destroying your capital. Thus, you will reduce all the amount of capital that you have in store to make trades. With passing time, all of this will tend to take a negative shape. It is mainly because it will be harder and harder for you to reoccupy all kinds of losses as the position size will also reduce, resulting from the reducing capital.

Not Paying Attention To Written Options

Writing options can turn out to be an effective way to generate income. It is because you will keep receiving the premium amount upfront while selling the options. Whenever an option expires worthless, you will get the chance to keep the overall received amount. The option premium is the maximum profit amount that you can earn. If the price of the security goes in the opposite direction to you, you will incur some huge loss. What is the mistake over here? The main mistake over here is that the option writer fails to lock up a portion of the premium as they get some chance to do so. If you think of selling options like gambling, you have highly mistaken. Getting into trade with the notion, "I wish my option expires worthless. I will get the chance to have all the premium," is not correct. You will have to get involved actively. You will have to realize the altering conditions. If you are 100% sure that an option is going to expire worthlessly, you can relax and just sit back.

However, if the outcome of an option is unclear to you, it will be better for you to close that position as early as possible. For instance, if you sell out put options at $2 and get out of the trade when the premium is $0.40, you will get the chance to have 80% of the premium that you have earned. It is a better option to keep the 80% compared to losing everything.

Chapter 10: Having The Right Mindset

The trading markets are neither moral nor immoral. To be precise, they are amoral. There is no form of emotion in the markets of trading. So, it will completely rely on you the way you will perceive the market. If your main target is to attain and maintain the successful status of a trader in the long run, it is essential to frame the right mindset. It will help you in observing the trading market from a kind of perspective where there is no existence of emotions. The kind of mindset you will have will be responsible for defining all your reactions as you lose trades and earn huge profits. A trader, who is successful, will never allow his/her emotions to play or interfere with the trading decisions. To achieve that, you will have to develop the right mindset. Regardless of the field in life, you are currently in, having a proper mindset will help you achieve all your goals and desires.

Improving Your Mindset

Improving your mindset is a necessity if you are willing to attain success in the trading world. You will have to follow certain strategies and tips that are simple and easy for doing this properly. You will get accustomed to all of them very easily. If you feel that your trading mindset needs some push for going up the ladder, here are some important tips for you. Learning these will help you to survive in the trading game.

Getting Into The Mindset Of A Trader

Traders can benefit to a great extent simply by approaching the trading market with a calm and relaxed mind. If you already have all the risk management guidelines in the perfect place, you are not required to worry about anything. What can go wrong, possibly? Even if a trade of yours reaches the stop-loss level, it is still not the end of the whole world. The game of trading is all about loss and profit. It will keep going on continuously. Even all those traders who are at the top of the success list have their winning only close to 50% than what you actually think. With a high reward-to-risk ratio, which is nothing but the overall ratio of potential profit or loss that might take place in a trade, you can still have some profit with a winning rate near to 50%.

When you lose any trade, it is not necessary to take it too personally. Trading markets move up and down continuously, every hour, every day. All that you will require to do is to have full confidence in your market analysis. In fact, fixing up a daily morning routine can help you to stay calm and relaxed while trading. Some strategies for improving concentration include waking up early, exercise or meditation, relaxing exercise, etc. The key is not to force your mind on a trade; just allow it to flow at its own pace.

Keep Learning

In this world, there is no definite end to learning. It is among all those factors that can separate successful traders from unsuccessful ones. Even after developing the right mindset, you will need to have some proper foundation of the markets to understand the sudden movements in the market along with the reason behind so. In short, you will have to understand the reactions of the market. There are several types of concepts in the trading world that are worth learning. It will always be for your own good if you can keep learning until you figure out the perfect tools that can suit your needs and style of trading properly.

You can opt for learning by reading a good trading book for one hour every day before going to bed to get a proper insight into all the famous practices of the successful traders. You can also opt for some effective online courses to improve your level of knowledge about the trading market. Just keep learning as much as possible. Learning is the only thing in this world that is never going to harm you.

Maintaining Trading Journal

A superb way to attain the proper mindset of a successful trader is by keeping a trading journal. Trading journals are similar to normal journals. The only difference between these two is that trading journals are all about the trading information that you opt for. It will include journal entries, which can literally cover anything that you think is beneficial for your trades. The common standard entries of the trading journal include your traded currency pair, your entry and exit points, reasons for getting into specific trades, and several other important commentaries regarding the trading market. Just after you successfully close a trade, make it your habit to update the trading journal of the same trade simply by filling up the related entries, along with the loss or profit of that trade. If you want, you can add extra comments as well that you think is an essential insight into the trade performance.

When you make it a habit to regularly maintain a trading journal, you can easily keep track of your trading patterns resulting in trade losses. It might also be that the majority of the trades made by you resulted in a loss. Your trading journal can provide you with the necessary insight about the same. Following this will help you to improve your trading skills so that losses can be minimized.

Keeping A Note That The Market Of Trading Does Not Owe You Anything

A primary mistake made by most of the traders is to overtrade a market continuously. It is specifically when a trade goes in the wrong direction; there are traders who keep chasing the market to get some trading opportunities. It will ultimately result in huge losses right at the end of the day. It is not how the trading market functions. The trading market doesn't owe anything to anyone. It will help you if you can repeat this idea after waking up in the morning every day. Do not get angry if you lose a trade. Always remember, the trading market does not have emotion of any kind, but you do.

Chapter 11: Psychology Of Trading

You will have to master several skills to be a successful trader in the market of trading. Such skills also include the power to evaluate the fundamentals of the concerned company and also determine the direction of the stock trend. However, no other skill is as important as the psychology of a trader. Having emotion, fast-thinking, and exercising the right discipline are some of the major components of what is collectively known as trading psychology. You will have to understand and keep control of two emotions: fear and greed.

Quick Decisions

The majority of the time, traders have to think quickly and also opt for fast decisions. Also, they need to dart in and out of the related stocks within a short period of time. To properly accomplish all these, you will have to develop a certain presence of mind. You will also need to maintain proper discipline to stick to your set trading plans. You will have to understand the perfect time for booking profits and losses. There is no other option to permit emotions to get in your way.

Understanding Fear

Whenever traders get some bad news regarding a specific stock or about an entire economy, they will have a natural tendency to get scared. Also, they might start overreacting to the situation and might also get the feeling of liquidating all the holdings that they possess. In such a situation, they would like to sit on their cash. They might not be able to gather the required strength for taking any other risk again. As a trader, you will have to properly understand the fear: a natural reaction that gets perceived to a threat. Right in this context, it is a threat to all the potential profits. However, quantification of fear can help. You will have to consider figuring out what you are actually scared of. Also, you will need to find out the reason behind the same. But this entire thinking needs to take place much before the occurrence of the loss or bad news, and not after or in the middle of it.

As you think about your fears properly with time, you will get an idea regarding how you perceive various events in an instinctive way. You will also come to know how you react to all of them. All this will permit you to move away from the emotional responses. Indeed, doing all this is not that easy. However, it is very important for the health of your trading portfolio.

Dealing With Greed

If you ever visit Wall Street, you will find a very old saying: Pigs get slaughtered. It actually refers to the greedy attitude of the investors to stick to a single position for a long time with the motive of winning. It also involves getting every tick in the upward direction of the price. However, within a very short period of time, the trend just gets reversed, and the greedy nature of the investor gets caught in a huge trap. Greed is not at all easy to deal with or fight over. It is completely based on the human instinct to do better and to get a little more than what you currently possess. As a successful trader, it is of prime importance to understand such an instinct and develop a proper trading plan which is based on a rational way of thinking. It does not involve any whims or instincts.

Developing Rules

It is necessary for a trader to develop a new set of rules and follow the same when the psychology crunch comes into play. You will have to set up various guidelines depending on the tolerance level of the risk-reward ratio. You will have to determine a fixed profit target. Follow this by putting stop loss right behind it to move your emotions out of the way. Also, you can also decide which nature of events, whether positive or negative earnings, will trigger your decision to sell or purchase any stock. It will be a good thing for you if you can set certain limits on the highest amount that you can actually win or lose in a day. After you have reached your target, take out all your money, and keep running. If your target of loss reaches its predetermined number, fold up your tent and return home.

Conclusion

Thank you for making it through to the end of the *Options Trading for Beginners*; let's hope it was very informative and was able to provide you with all of the necessary tools you need to reach your goals, whatever they may be.

As you have reached the end of this book, you must have noticed that it has been said many times that trading is not a complicated subject. It is either very easy or very difficult. It all depends on the way you see it. Options trading is just like any other primary form of trading. It involves its own set of strategies and tools that you have already learned from this guidebook. Getting a hold of all such strategies will help you in becoming the master of options trading. So, it can be said that it does not even matter whether you a beginner or an expert in options trading. It is open for all. The only thing that can help you going is to remember that regardless of what happens in the trade, never stop learning.

To guarantee a constant flow of income, along with financial stability, options trading is the most effective and safe form of trading. The target of this book is to help the beginner traders with all the basic strategies and tools so that they can also start making profits from the same.

Finally, if you found this guidebook useful in any way, a review on Amazon is always appreciated!

Remember to follow Gualtiero Favole on Amazon to not miss the next books in publication.

www.ingramcontent.com/pod-product-compliance
Lightning Source LLC
Chambersburg PA
CBHW070655220526

45466CB00001B/448